INVESTIGATORS

Jay Dix, M.D.
Medical Examiner
Boone County, Missouri
and
Associate Professor of Pathology
Department of Pathology
University of Missouri

with Mary Fran Ernst
Medicolegal Investigator
St. Louis County, Missouri
and
Assistant Professor of Pathology
Director of Medicolegal Education
Department of Pathology
St.Louis University, Missouri

CRC Press
Boca Raton London New York Washington, D.C.

RARITAN VALLEY COMMUNITY COLLEGE
EVELYN S. FIELD LIBRARY

Library of Congress Cataloging-in-Publication Data

Catalog record is available from the Library of Congress

This book contains information obtained from authentic and highly regarded sources. Reprinted material is quoted with permission, and sources are indicated. A wide variety of references are listed. Reasonable efforts have been made to publish reliable data and information, but the author and the publisher cannot assume responsibility for the validity of all materials or for the consequences of their use.

Neither this book nor any part may be reproduced or transmitted in any form or by any means, electronic or mechanical, including photocopying, microfilming, and recording, or by any information storage or retrieval system, without prior permission in writing from the publisher.

The consent of CRC Press LLC does not extend to copying for general distribution, for promotion, for creating new works, or for resale. Specific permission must be obtained in writing from CRC Press LLC for such copying.

Direct all inquiries to CRC Press LLC, 2000 N.W. Corporate Blvd., Boca Raton, Florida 33431.

Trademark Notice: Product or corporate names may be trademarks or registered trademarks, and are used only for identification and explanation, without intent to infringe.

Visit the CRC Press Web site at www.crcpress.com

© 1999 by CRC Press LLC

No claim to original U.S. Government works
International Standard Book Number 0-8493-0298-6
Printed in the United States of America   3 4 5 6 7 8 9 0
Printed on acid-free paper

Contents

Preface

In most jurisdictions, the body of a deceased individual and the death scene are the responsibilities of a medical examiner's (or coroner's) office and the local law enforcement agency. A medicolegal death investigator is a representative of the medical examiner or coroner and should be the most knowledgeable person about the cause and manner of death at the death scene. The death investigator should focus on the physical condition of the body at the scene. Scene information regarding injuries, trace evidence, identification, and estimation of time of death should be evaluated and recorded. This information is essential to the medical examiner or coroner in order that a proper determination of cause and manner of death can be made.

The importance of an investigation in any death cannot be over-emphasized. In many cases, the scene investigation is more important than the autopsy. A thorough and complete investigation commonly leads to the proper diagnosis of the cause and manner of death prior to an autopsy. The medical examiner and coroner cannot perform their duties without this vital information. Well-trained investigators are an integral part in any forensic jurisdiction. The importance of sound investigation will become more evident as the investigator uses this handbook.

Acknowledgments

I would like to thank Dr. John Townsend, Chairman of the Department of Pathology, University of Missouri, for allowing me to use departmental resources to complete this project. I am indebted to Kirstie Calcutt and Ardath Calvert for their help with the photographs. I would also like to thank Dr. Robert Calaluce who edited some of the material used in this handbook.

1

Guidelines for the Death Scene Investigator

1. Pre-plan the Death Investigation

When initially notified of a death, the death investigator should determine as much information as possible from the caller. Approximate age and sex will enable a subject to be placed in the appropriate "medical category." Determining where the decedent has been found will be helpful in investigational planning. An attempt should be made to ascertain if there is any evidence of foul play or if any implements are available that might have played a role in the subject's death. By gathering these pieces of death scene data, the death investigator will be able to anticipate additional information that may be needed upon arrival at a scene.

2. Establish Telephone Contact with the Death Scene

If notified by a dispatcher or another individual who is not on the scene, the investigator should attempt to contact a law enforcement officer or other official (i.e., coroner) at the death scene. By speaking directly with one of these individuals, additional information can be gained which will assist in planning necessary investigational scene activities. When speaking with this individual at the scene, a realistic expected arrival time should be provided.

3. Notification of Personnel Transporting the Remains

If possible, personally speak to the personnel who will be moving the decedent to the morgue. Explain the nature of the decedent's condition so they can be prepared if special handling is required (e.g., decomposition, infection, etc.). This information will be appreciated and will give the personnel additional time to prepare. The investigator is the best person to determine how much time before the body can be moved.

4. Cooperation Among Investigators

A successful death investigation involving more than one individual requires cooperation and coordination. Any potential conflicts should be worked out. Each office should have standard operating procedures which define the legal responsibilities for each investigating agency. Investigators from different agencies should meet prior to working scenes together so that potential areas of conflict can be discussed in an amicable and professional manner.

5. Photographs of Decedent at Death Scene

Usually, an agent from law enforcement will photograph the scene. This should be done prior to disturbing the scene or the deceased. A death investigator may also take photographs (Polaroid's are acceptable) for the forensic pathologist performing the autopsy. Information such as the location of the body and any unique circumstances at the death scene may help the pathologist. It is important to keep in mind the legal implications of the photographs. Will the photographs be able to be subpoenaed? Are they considered a part of the official medical examiner's enquiry? If a death investigator suspects a violent or suspicious death, law enforcement should be requested to take photographs.

6. Identification of the Deceased

Positive identification of the decedent is crucial in all death inquiries. The family should be notified. Information such as medical history, work, and social history can only be obtained after an identification is established. Care must be taken to ensure that the identification is absolutely correct.

7. Examination of the Body

A systematic and thorough inspection of the decedent should be performed by an investigator. A routine pattern of evaluation should be performed in each assessment. If an investigator always begins at the top of the subject's body and moves toward the feet, the possibility of missing important injuries or evidence is lessened.

The following should be described:

1. Any obvious injuries or abnormalities.
2. Rigor and livor mortis.
3. Body and environmental temperatures.
4. Environmental conditions such as moisture and wind.
5. Appropriateness of the clothing for type, size, and cleanliness.
6. Does it appear that the person has been redressed with buttons buttoned and zippers zipped.
7. Note all jewelry. Are any items missing?
8. Money and credit cards should be documented and returned to the legal next-of- kin.

No analyses, such as gunshot residue or fingerprinting, should be performed on the decedent's body at the scene without the expressed consent of the forensic pathologist responsible for the postmortem examination. Clothing should not be removed. The body should not be cleansed. No liquids or powders should be placed on the deceased as these might interfere with radiographs or chemical testing. If more than one hour has elapsed since the initial body assessment has been made, and the decedent is still at the scene, a second assessment (to include body temperature, rigor and livor mortis) should be recorded. A thorough body visualization at the scene gives an investigator the capability to differentiate injuries noted at the scene from any body injuries sustained during conveyance to the morgue.

8. Other Scene Information Collection

The investigator must also gather information that relates to the cause and manner of death. Each type of death requires specific scene information. For instance, questions to be asked in a motor vehicle fatality would not be the same as those asked in an autoerotic sexual asphyxial death. Since different questions need to be asked, an investigational guide for each specific type of death can be very useful.

9. Determine What Information Has Already Been Developed

Prior to the investigator's arrival, law enforcement officers, paramedics, and other support personnel have most likely already communicated with individuals or witnesses at the scene. An investigator needs to know this initial information so that he can compare initial data with the decedent's body data and determine if there are any discrepancies. It is better to ask the question twice and get the same answer, than to accept as fact information that has been checked by one source. The investigator needs to determine, for instance, why the body information (rigor, livor, temperature, clothing, injuries, etc.) differs from the witness information.

10. Collect Evidence Items That May Have Contributed to the Subject's Death

Evidence confiscation authority is clearly defined. Any item that is on or attached to the decedent belongs to the medicolegal death investigator. Any item found at the scene (not on or attached to the decedent) is under the control of the law enforcement agency. Any weapon or other item possibly related to the death found at the scene should be made available to the pathologist. Often, substances are the causative agent in the death. Be sure to confiscate all medication and alcoholic beverage containers. Note the location where each item was found. Studies have shown that the fatal intoxicant is likely to be found in the same room or location as the decedent. Drug paraphernalia, notes, or any unusual item that might have been used by or written by the subject should be confiscated. All evidence should be appropriated during the initial investigation because the investigator may not return and recover any items without the permission of the owner once the scene has been relinquished.

11. Interviews Regarding the Death

Standard operating procedure of the jurisdiction dictates who should be interviewed and by whom. Interviews should include basic information such as the subject's identification, clothing, time, date, and state of wellness when last seen alive, date and time the body was discovered, and medical, employment, and social history. Also important are any recent events that may have a bearing on the death. A death investigator should always ask if the decedent had recently been involved in any potentially harmful situations. This information may be extremely helpful if later attempts are made to make a prior incident a contributing factor in the death. If suicide is suspected, it is preferable to interview family members and close friends as soon as possible after the death is discovered. This may preclude guilt-related, subconscious, erroneous statements made by loved ones several days later.

12. Transporting the Body

A decedent should not sustain additional injuries or be tampered within the time he is removed from leaves the death scene and is inspected by the pathologist. An investigator can help alleviate many potential problems by being present during the movement of a subject from the scene to the morgue. Safeguarding the decedent and trace evidence can be accomplished by placing subjects in clean white sheets or body bags. These should be brought to the scene by the death investigator or members of the office. Do not use any materials from the scene in order to avoid any possible contamination with trace evidence at the scene. Trace evidence on extremities can be safeguarded by use of previously unused paper bags secured by tape. If the head is quite fragile, it can be encased in a large fresh paper bag. Careful attention should be paid to locating projectiles that might be loosely caught in the decedent's hair or clothing. Be sure to look under the decedent after the body has been moved to see if any item has been left behind.

The investigator is responsible for the decedent until the body is placed on the examining table and should therefore be familiar with all persons who come in contact with the decedent at the scene. Any problems regarding the careful and respectful handling of the subject or safeguarding of valuables should be immediately controlled by an investigator.

13. Pronouncement of Death

A jurisdiction's law dictates who can perform this function. Many paramedical personnel will not pronounce an individual dead for fear of associated legal problems. A definite pronouncement date, place, and time is required for completion of a death certificate. This information should always be clearly stated in an investigator's death report.

Problems may arise when a subject is found in a decomposed state, since death most probably did not occur on the day that the decedent was discovered. Noting that the date of death is actually the "date of discovery" may solve this dilemma. Also, the problem of survivorship can occur when two persons (usually spouses) die as a result of the same incident. If possible, it is important to note, for insurance purposes, who expired first.

14. Family Notification

The most unpleasant task in a death investigation is probably notifying a family of a sudden, unexpected death. It is often an investigator's responsibility. There is no easy way to accomplish this task. Family reaction to this news is based upon many different things: cultural norms, recent family closeness, guilt, and a subject's place within the family structure. It is important that the family be notified of the death only when an investigator is absolutely positive of the identification of the victim. If the identification is not solidly based on scientific evidence (dental exam, fingerprints, or radiographic comparison), then caution must be exercised in declaring the positive identification. When subjects are in the state of decomposition, thermally injured, or physically mutilated, the investigator should resist the temptation to accept personal papers or visual identification as the sole source of identification information. If a body is misidentified, then two identification errors have been made: a suspected dead person may be alive and a suspected living person is dead.

The decedent must be positively identified before the name is released to the news media. The next-of-kin must be notified prior to releasing the name to the media.

15. The Investigative Report

This document should contain information from each of the sections addressed above. The report should be in a form that can easily be understood by forensic professionals and laymen. It should be accurate, with proper grammar and correct spelling, and written in chronological order. This report will be utilized by many professionals within the department and from outside agencies. An investigator should carefully check the report before it is released. Remember that the report reflects the professional competence of the investigator.

2

Signs of Sudden Death and Disease

Position of the Body

The investigator should not be concerned if the decedent's body is discovered in an apparently uncomfortable or unusual position. The decedent may be found lying in a contorted position on the floor in any room of the house, especially the bedroom and the bathroom. As a rule, the more twisted the position, the more sudden the death. This doesn't mean a victim of sudden death may not die in bed. Many times the decedent may have become ill and made it to the bathroom or their bed and died in an apparently comfortable position.

The most common cause of a sudden collapse is heart disease. When the heart begins to beat fast and irregularly (called an arrhythmia), the victim can collapse within seconds or less. The arrhythmia may occur at anytime without warning. Victims may collapse in bed, in the bathroom, while reading the newspaper, or walking down the street. An arrhythmia may also occur during times of stress, such as when shoveling snow or after a traffic accident.

Blood at the Scene

Any disease that causes a rapid loss of blood may cause sudden death. Obviously, trauma such as a gunshot wounds, stabbings, and blunt trauma can cause sudden death from bleeding, but these rarely present a problem in interpretation for the investigator. Abundant blood at the

9

scene does not necessarily mean foul play. The investigator needs to observe the location of the blood and the degree of or lack of spattering. Abundant blood spattering usually indicates trauma to the body with blood being thrown around, especially if the spattering is located high on the walls or ceiling.

Natural deaths may be associated with abundant blood near or away from the body. Chronic alcoholics may have such advanced disease that they may bleed from the mouth or the rectum or both. This is caused by liver damage (cirrhosis) in which blood begins to back up in the veins of the esophagus and the rectum. These thick and swollen veins are called varices. Varices have a tendency to rupture, and when they do, the bleeding may be quite extensive. The decedent may die within minutes, although the time is usually longer. There may be abundant blood in the toilet, bathtub, on towels, or in cups.

Vomitus

One common problem when dealing with sudden death concerns the interpretation of the presence of vomitus on the face. Many investigators have learned incorrectly that vomitus is an indication the decedent aspirated or choked on the vomitus and this is likely the cause of death. Or they conclude the aspiration at least played a part in the person's death. It is true that aspiration may play a part in a person's death, but this is rarely true when dealing with a sudden death. The presence of vomitus usually means nothing more than the decedent vomited as death was occurring.

Vomiting may also occur in the final process of dying when the decedent is unconscious for a considerable period such as under the influence of alcohol or other drugs. In this circumstance, the individual is unconscious long enough that vomitus is breathed back down into the lungs and an infection of the lungs (pneumonia) develops. The pneumonia which develops is rarely very impressive to the naked eye at the autopsy table and is usually considered to be a secondary factor when determining the cause of death.

Vomitus may cause suspicious-looking marks on the face and neck. Stomach acid may cause abrasions of the skin. These superficial injuries may appear as if the decedent ingested a caustic solution.

Froth and/or Blood in the Nose and Mouth

This is commonly scene in cases of sudden infant death syndrome (SIDS). Fluid from the lungs comes up the airway and may exude from the nose and mouth. This should not be considered a suspicious sign of death even if there is a large amount soaked into the bedding. Blood may mix with the air or agonal (at death) breathing to produce the froth or bubbles. The froth may be quite bloody, or white if there is no blood.

This does not mean that all froth, either bloody or not, is a sign of natural disease. Froth may be an indication of a drug overdose, or drowning. Many drug overdoses cause depression of breathing which leads to lung failure and death. Fluid builds up in the lungs and airways.

Medications at the Scene

Insight into a person's medical history can be gained by looking at the types of medicine a person was or should have been taken. Medicines for heart disease, seizures or other diseases may indicate a potential cause of sudden death. Not only will the types of pills be on the container, but the name of the prescribing physician and pharmacy will also be present. A listing of medicines commonly found at the scene can be found in Appendix B.

External Signs of Disease or Trauma

General

Marked congestion (blood pooling) of the head and upper chest — Congestion means an accumulation of blood. When the head and chest appear dark purple then they are said to be congested because blood has backed up into these areas. This an indication the heart has failed, usually suddenly. The most common cause is heart disease, especially coronary artery disease, however, any type of heart disease may cause this finding. Other diseases such as seizures, pulmonary thromboemboli (blood clots in the lungs) and asthma to name a few can cause this process. Unnatural causes such as an overdose or suffocation may also be the cause.

Jaundice — This is yellowish discoloration of the skin which can be seen in either liver disease, infection (septicemia), or the breakdown of blood. The whites of the eyes may be yellow (icterus) and be the first sign of this process.

Bruising — This is a sign of trauma, however, all bruises should not be considered suspicious. Elderly individuals bruise easily and they usually have areas of bleeding (ecchymoses) on the forearms and hands. This does not mean the individual was abused by someone else.

Unkempt condition — General uncleanliness may be due to alcoholism, drug abuse, or a mental disorder.

Condition of the clothing — The type of clothing may help indicate the time of death.

Living conditions — The condition of the apartment or house may give an indication of alcoholism or drug abuse. Of course, the person could just be a slob.

Muscle wastage — (see Cachexia).

Cachexia — Generalized muscle wastage; the "concentration camp" look. This may be seen in any end stage (terminal) chronic disease. However, this appearance should not be present in someone not expected to appear as such. This is a sign of malnutrition which does not occur without a reason. Unless there is an adequate explanation, this change should not be present in children or an elderly person without disease.

Hypopigmented areas — These are either signs of skin disease (loss of pigmentation in dark-skinned individuals) or old trauma, such as burns.

Raised lesions — Cancer, or more often, benign nodules.

Dark and flat skin lesions — Kaposi's sarcoma (cancer) in AIDS, melanoma (cancer), or benign moles.

Bleeding in the skin and tissues — Bruising from trauma (alcoholics, and older people bleed easily. The elderly commonly have bleeding under the skin (ecchymoses) on the forearms. Minor trauma will cause these. Other bruises may be caused by intentional or accidental abuse.

Spider angiomata — Small areas of dilated blood vessels seen most often in alcoholics.

Head

Unequal pupils (anisocoria) — The pupils may be unequal because of head trauma or may only be an incidental finding.

Loss of clumps of hair (alopecia) — Natural disease, such as stress, or abuse.

Petechiae — Pinpoint hemorrhages of the eyes, eyelids, face or upper chest. Not to be confused with

Tardieu spots which occur with long term settling of blood. Petechiae of the eyes suggests suffocation, however, sudden death from heart disease can cause them. Petechiae of the face, neck, and chest suggests a compression asphyxiation.

Poor dentition — Poor hygiene, seen in chronic alcoholism, drug abuse, or low socioeconomic conditions.

Swollen parotid glands — On the side of the face; due to chronic alcoholism.

Blood emanating from the nose mouth — Trauma or bleeding from bleeding of the stomach or esophagus from cancer or alcoholism.

Blue lips — Heart or lung disease.

Sunken eyes — Dehydration; also associated with tenting (skin doesn't return to normal when pulled).

Extremities

Clubbing of the fingers — This is a rounding of the fingertips due to lung disease.

Arthritis — Joint swelling, especially of the fingers. Look for ulnar deviation (bending of the fingers towards the little finger).

Extremities of different sizes — Swelling from the formation of a blood clot.

Obvious deformities — Old injuries (such as fractures) or congenital abnormalities.

Swollen ankles — Heart failure. The degree of swelling is judged by the "pitting" of the skin when pressed by a finger.

Lower leg skin discoloration and a loss of hair — Lack of blood flow to the legs due to poor circulation.

Caused by either blood vessel disease, such as diabetes, or heart failure.

Fingernails and toenails — They become thickened and yellow with age.

Trunk

Enlarged breasts in men (gynecomastia) — Liver damage (alcoholism) causing an increase in estrogen.

Protuberance of the abdomen — This must be differentiated from general obesity, air from CPR, and fluid accumulation from disease (i.e., blood or fluid from ruptures or liver disease).

Barrel-shaped chest — Chronic emphysema.

Tense (tight) abdomen — Accumulated blood or fluid in the peritoneal cavity. It may be from a natural process such as alcoholism or cancer or trauma.

Blood emanating from the anus — Cancer or rupture of blood vessels complicating alcoholism.

Skin

Brown spots (not raised) — Senile (old-age) changes, especially of the hands, face, and forearms.

Raised soft brown lesions (seborrheic keratoses) — Benign nodules commonly seen in the elderly.

Raised red-brown scaly firm lesions — These are actinic keratoses which are caused by the sun and may be precancerous

Raised uncolored bumps — Sebaceous glands or infected hair follicles - benign.

Red spots — Small groups of blood vessels, usually normal.

Skin is pale — Anemia (lack of blood from excessive bleeding or poor nutrition).

Yellow palms and soles — Excessive carotene (yellow pigment), not traumatic.

3

Obtaining a Medical History

Speaking to medical professionals may not always be easy for the investigator. Most physicians and nurses who report a case to the Medical Examiner's Office are very helpful. Unfortunately, some are not. Some pick up on the investigator's lack of medical training and quickly lose patience with them. For some reason, if you are not in the "medical club," you are considered an outsider.

Investigations must be given the necessary information for the death report. Persistence will pay off in gaining insight into the past medical history. If the physician doesn't remember the patient, a request must be made for someone to review the chart (usually done by a nurse or secretary in the office). If the death occurred in a medical facility, the investigator may need to personally review the medical chart or obtain a copy for the pathologist.

Physicians may not fully understand that the pathology or diseases which cause sudden death as are seen in the field of forensic pathology and death investigation. They generally have received a few hours of lectures or training in medical school concerning sudden death. Therefore, it may be best to gather all the information and to be wary of the physician's opinion about the cause of death. Of course, the physician may know if the decedent was near death because of a terminal disease.

There is no way a lay investigator is expected, or can be expected, to know all the medical disorders dealing with sudden death, however, most of the diseases causing sudden death and medical terminology should be understood.

It is beyond the scope of this handbook to teach all of the causes of natural and traumatic death. In addition to reading textbooks, the information can be obtained from pathologists. Most pathologists will explain the causes and mechanisms of sudden death while they are performing autopsies. It behooves the investigator to attend autopsies and avail themselves to this information.

Reviewing Medical Charts

Occasionally, the investigator must personally review a medical char,. but rarely does the entire medical chart need to be reviewed in order to understand the diseases and death of a patient. The most important information can usually be obtained from the following:

1. **Discharge summary.** A summary of everything done to the patient and how the patient presented to the hospital. It will also tell about the death or the condition of the patient when discharged and the medications the patient was receiving. If the person dies in the hospital, the discharge summary may not have been typed before the information is needed. If not available, the physician should be contacted.

2. **Physician's notes.** Brief summaries of the day-to-day progress of the patient and what the physician thinks about the patient's course during hospitalization.

3. **Nurse's notes.** Shift notes. They may be the best indicator of how the patient was doing at a particular time of the day. Nurses make many notes during the day of the patient's progress, while a physician may only write one note during each day, if that often.

4

Traumatic Deaths

Firearms

Handguns and rifles fire ammunition or cartridges composed of a primer, gunpowder or propellant, and a bullet or projectile. When a firing pin of a weapon strikes the primer, the resulting explosion ignites the gunpowder. Gunpowder, vaporized primer, and metal from a gun may be deposited on skin and/or clothing of the victim. In addition, elements from the primer may be deposited on objects in close proximity to a discharged weapon.

Gunpowder comes out of the muzzle in two forms:

1. Completely burned gunpowder, called "soot" or "fouling", can be washed off the skin.
2. Particles of burning and unburned powder can become embedded in the skin or bounce off and abrade the skin. The marks on the skin are called "tattooing" or "stippling".

The presence or absence of gunpowder on the clothing or skin indicates whether the gunshot was contact (loose or tight), close, intermediate, or distant.

Tight contact — All gunpowder residue is on the edges or in the depths of a wound. There may be searing or burning of wound margins or reddening of surrounding skin due to carbon monoxide gas produced by burning powder. There is often tearing of the skin around the entrance wound in head wounds because of pressure buildup and blow-back of the skin towards the muzzle.

Loose contact — Gunpowder may escape from the barrel and be deposited around the edges of a wound.

Close range — Close range gunshot wounds occur at muzzle-to-target distances of approximately 6 to 12 inches. Both fouling and stippling are present.

Intermediate range — These wounds occur at muzzle-to- target distances of approximately 12 inches to 3 feet. There is no fouling, only stippling or deposition of particles on clothing.

Distant wounds — No fouling or stippling.

Entrance and exit wounds are generally easy to differentiate. Entrance wounds tend to be circular defects with a thin rim of abrasion caused by a bullet scraping and perforating the skin. Entrance wounds of the face can be quite atypical appearing because the surfaces are not flat.

Exit wounds may be circular like entrance wounds, but they are often irregular in shape. They may be slit-like or have ragged edges. They do not have a rim of abrasion-like entrance wounds unless a victim's skin is pressed against another object. This is called a "shored" exit wound. Skin around an exit wound may also be discolored because of underlying bleeding in the soft tissues.

The scene must be examined for bullets and cartridges. Bullets may be caught in clothing after exiting the body.

Shotguns

Shotguns have smooth bores. This means that a particular weapon cannot be matched to pellets recovered at a scene or from a body. The range of fire is determined similarly to handguns and rifles except the degree of pellet spread can be more helpful.

Shotguns usually fire pellets, but they can also fire slugs. These solid projectiles are similar to large bullets except they do not travel as far and usually stop in the target.

Cutting and Stabbing

Cutting (Incised) Wounds

An incised wound (cut) is made by a sharp instrument and is longer on the skin surface than it is deep. The edges of the wound are sharp and are usually not ragged or abraded. The surrounding skin is usually undamaged. Within the wound, tissue bridges do not connect one side to the other, as seen in lacerations.

Stab Wounds

A stab wound is deeper than it is wide. The size of a skin defect rarely gives an indication of the depth of a stab wound. The ends of the stab wound are the angles. The angles of the wound may be blunt or sharp depending on the weapon. A single-edged blade will create one blunt angle and one sharp angle. Knives with two cutting surfaces will cause two sharp angles. Homemade sharpened weapons may produce wounds having either sharp or dull angles.

The width and length of a weapon's blade may be determined by analyzing a stab wound. A 1/2-inch wide blade, for example, will cause a 1/2-inch wide wound on the skin surface if a knife is inserted and removed straight. If either the victim or assailant moves, the external wound may be longer. An external wound may also be slightly shorter because of the skin's elasticity. The depth of the wound track may be longer than the length of the blade because skin and surrounding tissues will collapse and spring back as the pressure is relieved.

Multiple incised and/or stab wounds of the neck, face, and extremities (so-called "defense" wounds) are usually caused by an assailant. Multiple incised wounds of varying depths on the neck or wrists suggest a suicide. Superficially incised wounds adjacent to a major incised wound are referred to as hesitation marks and are characteristic of self-inflicted injuries. A body sustaining tens or hundreds of stab and incised wounds is characteristic of a situation known as "overkill" which usually occurs in a highly emotional setting such as one involving sexual and/or drugs.

Asphyxia (Suffocation)

Asphyxia means death due to lack of oxygen to the brain. The following are the different ways a person can asphyxiate:

1. Compression of the neck (hanging and strangulation).

2. Blockage of the airway (suffocation, gagging).

3. Compression of the chest (postural asphyxia).

4. Chemical and lack of available oxygen.

Compression of the Neck

In hanging (usually suicide), the neck can be compressed by rope, wire, or articles of clothing. Pressure on the neck will usually occlude the vasculature, but not necessarily the airway (larynx or trachea). Very little pressure is needed to occlude the blood vessels. It is a misconception that the airway must be occluded to asphyxiate. Ruptured blood vessels in the tissues from prolonged hanging, especially in the lower extremities, are called Tardieu spots.

The neck can also be compressed manually by strangulation or throttling. An assailant must compress either the airway or the blood vessels to render a victim unconscious. The time it takes to render an individual unconscious is quite variable (seconds to over a minute). Once a victim becomes unconscious, pressure must be continued in order to cause death.

Signs of trauma to the neck are generally evident in manual strangulation and hanging. There may be contusions or abrasions but rarely lacerations. An object used to compress the neck often leaves an abraded, imprinted mark. If the ligature is thin like a rope, the depressed mark on the neck is usually apparent and the pattern can be matched to the particular ligature. If the ligature is wide like a towel or shirt there will be no specific pattern of the ligature. There may superficial fingernail cuts from either the victim or assailant, however they are usually from the victim.

Pinpoint hemorrhages, or petechiae, are commonly present in the eyes after manual compression of the neck. Petechiae may be on either the bulb of the eye or on the lids or both. Petechiae may also be found on the face, especially the forehead, and around the eyes. They are caused by the buildup of vascular pressure which causes capillaries to rupture. They are not often found in suicidal hanging. Petechiae are not specific for asphyxiation and may occur in sudden natural death.

Autoerotic Deaths

A unique subgroup of asphyxial deaths are autoerotic deaths which occur during purposeful attempts to reduce blood flow to the brain by neck compression during masturbation. Any object which compresses the neck can be used. Most of the time a towel or some soft object is placed between the ligature and the neck to prevent visible scrapes or bruises. The diagnosis is readily made at the scene because the decedent may be naked, and pornographic material is usually found nearby. Often there is evidence of repeated behavior at the scene, such as grooves worn in the rafters where ropes or pulleys have been placed. The manner of death is accidental.

Blockage of the Airway (Suffocation, Aspiration, Gagging)

If the airway is blocked then oxygen cannot get into the lungs and asphyxiation results. A pillow or hand, for instance, can be placed over the mouth, prevent a person from breathing, and cause suffocation. An unchewed peanut or small parts of toys can become lodged in the airway of and infant or child. Individuals without teeth or with a history of stroke or other debilitating disease may have trouble chewing and may aspirate food into the airway. Those under the influence of alcohol are also more likely to aspirate. There are usually no signs of trauma in these deaths.

Compression of the Chest (Postural Asphyxia)

Postural asphyxiation occurs when a person cannot breathe because of an inability to move one's chest. This type of circumstance is commonly seen during motor vehicle accidents when the vehicle overturns on a victim or a driver may become trapped between the steering wheel and seat. There may be surprisingly few injuries except for other signs of blunt trauma.

Chemical and Lack of Available Oxygen

If the oxygen in the atmosphere is replaced by another chemical or gas, or if a person's red blood cells are unable to deliver oxygen to bodily tissues, a person will asphyxiate. Depletion of atmospheric oxygen usually occurs in a relatively closed environment. Examples include gas which can accumulate and displace oxygen in improperly vented mine shafts, sewers, or chemical storage tanks. It is common to encounter multiple deaths in such cases because rescuers can also be overcome by fumes and lack of oxygen.

Examples of chemical asphyxia by interfering with oxygen delivery to the tissues include carbon monoxide and cyanide. When a car is left running in a closed garage, carbon monoxide from burning gasoline competes with oxygen on the red blood cells. Carbon monoxide can incapacitate a person very quickly. Cyanide causes livor mortis to be red as in carbon monoxide poisoning. The cyanide gas may smell like bitter almonds. Both deaths can occur quickly, especially cyanide poisoning.

Drowning

The diagnosis of drowning is one of exclusion. There are no good drowning tests to prove a person drowned and an autopsy is inconclusive. The body is usually wet or is found in water to make the diagnosis. There may be injuries from being in the water, such as tears and scrapes of the skin from impacts against boats or bridges. Occasionally, marine life, more often in salt water, may feed on the skin of the face, especially around the mouth, nose, and ears. Abrasions may be found on the forehead, knees, and backs of hands from the body scraping against the bottom of the lake or pool. There may be no external signs of trauma. Froth in the nose and mouth may be present. Wrinkling of the skin on the hands and feet is typical.

Electrocution

Electrocution is not always an easy diagnosis to make. The history and circumstances of death are vitally important because low-voltage deaths frequently cause no injuries on the body. On the other hand, high-voltage deaths are easier to diagnose because of obvious burns.

The cause of death from electrocution is related to the amount of current (or amperage) flowing through a body. Although both direct and alternating currents can be lethal, most deaths occur from contact with alternating currents having low voltages such as 110 or 220 usually found in homes.

There needs to be a complete circuit from the power source to the ground for death to occur. A person will not become electrocuted if insulated from the ground. The direction the path takes in the body determines whether shock will be fatal. An arrhythmia is likely if current travels through the heart.

External injuries may vary tremendously. The extent of external wound damage is dependent upon the amount of current and its duration. If a current is spread over a wide contact area for a short duration there will not be any injuries to the skin. Clothing may be damaged so it must be retained for examination. The skin may be secondarily injured by burning clothes.

Low voltage tends to cause easily overlooked small burns especially on the hands and the feet. The lesions may be red, black, or white and inconspicuous, with depressed firm white centers. High-voltage deaths usually leave easily recognizable, deeply charred areas. Lesions may be present at the entrance and/or exit sites.

If a death occurs due to working with electrical equipment, the equipment will need to be tested by a qualified individual.

Lightning

Lightning may kill by either a direct or an indirect strike. Injuries may be slight to nonexistent or quite impressive. The victim usually dies by heart stoppage. Metal on the clothing or body may heat up and cause secondary injuries. Occasionally, a red, fern-like pattern may develop on the skin. This is only seen in electrocution and may disappear within hours of the death.

Fire Deaths and Thermal Injuries

Most fire deaths are due to carbon monoxide (CO) poisoning, not direct thermal injury. Exposure to CO can be fatal within minutes. Thermal effects to the body may be slight or severe. The degree of heat does not dictate how long a person survives during a fire. The extent of damage depends on the length of time a decedent is exposed to flames and how close a body is to a fire.

The most important factor in any fire death investigation is determining whether an individual was dead before a fire started (suspected homicide). This is determined by examining the airway for the inhalation of smoke and the measurement of CO content in the blood. These evaluations can only be determined in the morgue.

CO will cause cherry red livor mortis. Occasionally the CO will be negative as is in an explosion which causes death rapidly. A negative CO might initially be confusing, but a quality scene investigation should resolve any problems.

Individuals may die later in the hospital from complications such as inhalation injuries to the airways, infections.

and fluid and electrolyte disorders. Skin burns may range from partial or full thickness to charring and incineration.

Heat artifacts include:

1. Changes in height and weight of the body.
2. Changes in hair color. Brown hair may become red and blonde may become gray. Black hair does not change color.
3. Thermal fractures. These are difficult to differentiate from antemortem fractures.
4. Skin splits with evisceration of organs.

Most fire deaths should be x-rayed so that foreign objects will not be overlooked. Blood can usually be obtained from a body regardless of how badly it is burned.

Hyperthermia

Very few signs at autopsy will indicate a person died from hyperthermia. The most important sign is body temperature. If a body is found at a scene soon after death, an increased temperature will be evident. If a decedent is not found for many hours, or is discovered the next day, a diagnosis may be impossible.

There are a number of causes of hyperthermia. Older people may succumb to heat during summer months because of an underlying disease which contributes to their inability to cope with heat, or their dwellings may not have an appropriate cooling system. Malignant hyperthermia is a syndrome which develops in people who react to certain drugs, such a phenathiozines (thorazine) or halothane. The use of cocaine and methamphetamine are also associate with hyperthermia. In some of these cases there is a genetic predisposition toward developing "malignant" hyperthermia.

Hypothermia

Hyporthermia occurs more commonly in those individuals who have underlying disease or are incapacitated, such as under the influence of alcohol. People can die from improperly heated homes or apartments or if they are caught outside in the cold. Alcoholics can become hypothermic if they fall asleep in the cold while inebriated. Nursing-home patients can succumb to the cold after becoming confused and walk outdoors during winter months.

There are usually no external signs of trauma unless the individual was rendered incapacitated by an injury before dying from the cold.

"Paradoxical undressing" may occur because the individual may begin to undress while dying from the cold. This may appear suspicious if the decedent is a naked woman found outside with her clothes strewn about. An initial impression may suggest sexual assault, however, further investigation should uncover the correct manner and cause of death.

Blunt Trauma

General

The characteristic injuries of blunt trauma are contusions, abrasions, and lacerations. Abrasions occur externally whereas contusions and lacerations may be external or internal.

Contusions (Bruises)

Contusions are discolorations of the skin caused by bleeding into the tissues from ruptured blood vessels. In general, the older a person, the easier the vessels will rupture. There is no way, however, to determine exactly how much force is needed to produce a contusion. The age of a contusion is difficult to determine because of the great variability of a body's reaction to trauma. People with blood disorders and liver disease may develop more severe contusions than healthy individuals. As healing occurs, a contusion changes color from blue or red, to red-blue, to green, to brown, and finally yellow. These color changes, however, may appear out of order and may overlap. There is no way to know how long each color stage will last. Occasionally a recent contusion will have a brown tinge.

Abrasions (Scrapes)

An abrasion is denuded skin caused by friction. A wound may be either deep or superficial depending on the force and the coarseness of the surface which caused the abrasion. A person who slides across pavement might have a deeper and rougher wound than a person who slides across a rug. Occasionally, the direction of the force can be determined. For example, if one end of a wound has margins with raised skin, the force originated from the opposite side.

Lacerations (Tears)

Tears of the skin from blunt trauma are called lacerations. Many tears are associated with both contusions and abrasions. For example, a blow to the head with a hammer may cause tearing of the scalp with adjacent abrasions. If blood escapes into the surrounding tissues, the skin can also be bruised.

A laceration must be distinguished from a cutting injury. A laceration usually has bridges of tissue connecting one side of the wound to the other. Cutting and incised wounds have no tissue bridges because a sharp object cuts the wound cleanly from the top to the bottom of the wound.

Deaths due to blunt trauma may have some or none of the above external signs of trauma. This is particularly true of fatal blows to the abdomen.

Motor Vehicle Occupant Injuries

When a motor vehicle is involved in an accident, the driver and passengers will travel toward the site of the impact. For example, an impact to the front left of a car during a head-on crash will cause occupants to move to the left, especially if unrestrained. The driver may hit the steering wheel, dashboard or windshield, and the passenger the dashboard, windshield or rear-view mirror. Each may have significant injuries even though they hit different objects.

There may be few external marks when there are seat belts and airbags, however, internally, there may be impressive injuries to the heart and aorta. Seat belt abrasions on the shoulder and hips are common. The location of the marks help differentiate between the driver and the passenger.

Side-window glass causes a characteristic injury because it is made of tempered glass which will shatter into numerous small fragments upon impact. These fragments will cause a characteristic "dicing" pattern of lacerated abrasions on the face, shoulders, or arms. A driver will have dicing injuries on the left side of the body and a passenger will have them on the right.

Other common injuries involve fractures of the patella (knee) and femur caused by hitting the dashboard and the extremities caught under the seat. High-speed collisions can cause multiple severe injuries. There may be extensive skull fractures and facial lacerations, contusions, and abrasions. Common injuries to the trunk include rib and pelvic fractures with associated internal injuries. Lacerations of these internal organs may occur without associated rib fractures. If any of the occupants are ejected during a crash, obviously the injuries may be quite variable and very severe. Head trauma is common in these situations. In addition, when an occupant is ejected, a vehicle may roll over and compress the occupants, causing compressive asphyxia, often with few other injuries.

Pedestrian Injuries

In a hit-and-run fatality, a study of the injuries may help identify the vehicle. The points of impact on a body are particularly important and clothing must be closely examined for paint chips and parts of the vehicle that may be transferred on impact. Bumper impact sites on the legs should be measured from the heel. This may indicate the bumper height. A bumper fracture is often triangular in shape with the apex of the triangle pointing in the direction that a vehicle was moving. If a driver applied the brakes suddenly, a bumper fracture may be lower than expected because applying the brakes may drop the front end of the car. Adults tend to be run under while children with a lower centers of gravity tend to be run over.

Blunt Head Trauma

Blunt trauma to the scalp and face can produce contusions, lacerations, and abrasions. However, there may be no external signs of trauma to the head if a person has a full head of hair. Obvious external injuries are not necessary for a death to be caused by head trauma.

Battle's sign — bluish discoloration of the skin behind the ear that occurs from blood leaking under the scalp after a skull fracture.

Spectacle hemorrhage (raccoon' eyes) — discoloration of the tissues around the eyes due to a fracture of the skull. The hemorrhages may involve one or both eyes and may be mistakenly interpreted that the decedent had been struck about the face and eyes.

Pediatric Forensic Pathology

Investigation fatalities in children requires special expertise because injury patterns are different than in adults and may be quite subtle. Children who are repeatedly battered may present with multiple types and ages of injuries. Some may have no visible external injuries but have fatal organ damage internally, such as a ruptured liver. There may be few or no injuries to the head as in the case of a baby who is violently shaken.

Essential to a correct diagnosis in all infant deaths is the history. The medical personnel who first see these children and interact with the families have the best opportunity to find out from the caregiver what occurred. All statements should be recorded shortly after they have been made. Frequently, the history of how an injury occurred is inconsistent with the pattern and type of injury discovered by the pathologist.

Battered Child Syndrome

These children have a history of being repeatedly beaten by a caregiver. The injuries occur over a period of weeks, months, and years. Usually there are numerous injuries of different ages. It is common to see a child with healing rib fractures and old contusions in addition to the recent injuries which caused death. The external injuries to the head from blunt trauma may only be visible on the undersurface of the scalp. Contusions of the trunk may be readily apparent or absent even though there are fatal injuries to the internal organs.

All injuries should be photographed. Signs of sexual abuse will be determined by the pathologist.

Shaken Baby Syndrome

Shaking a child or an infant may cause a fatal head injury without external marks. Violent shaking may cause nerve damage, brain swelling, and slight hemorrhage. Retinal hemorrhages may also occur, but these can only be seen with an ophthalmoscope. There may be contusions on the arms or chest where the infant was grabbed while being shaken.

A child usually becomes unconscious or noticeably abnormal within minutes of the violent act. Since there may be no obvious signs of abuse, emergency room personnel may not be suspicious of any foul play. An investigation should be conducted on any child who is dead on arrival or dies in the emergency room.

If a child dies in an emergency room the scene of injury should be visited and investigated.

Neglect

Children do not need to be battered with multiple internal and external injuries for a medical examiner to rule the death a homicide. Child abuse and death can result from neglect. For example, if a child is not fed or if a child is left in a harmful situation (like a hot car), death may occur.

If a child is malnourished, his skin may be lax with little underlying soft tissue. He may appear underweight for his age, and the eyes may appear sunken. Vitreous humor will be sampled later at autopsy for chemical confirmation of dehydration. Sudden loss of weight can be determined by reviewing any previous medical records and comparing past to present weights.

Sudden Infant Death Syndrome (Crib Death)

A diagnosis of SIDS requires a complete autopsy and scene investigation and can only be diagnosed if both the scene and the autopsy are unremarkable. There is no provable cause of death.

Questions and observations of the scene:

1. Sleeping conditions. Was the child sleeping with the parents, in their bed or in his own crib?

2. Were there soft pillows or conditions in which the child could have suffocated on bedding or in between parts of the crib, bed, or other furniture?

3. When was the child last seen and fed?

4. There may be bloody fluid exuding from the mouth. This is commonly seen in a SIDS death.

5. Do the caretaker's statements fit the body? Are livor and rigor appropriate for the reported times given?

5

Time of Death and Decomposition

Time of Death (Postmortem Interval)

The determination of time of death, or the interval between the time of death and when the body is found (i.e., postmortem interval), can only be estimated unless there is a witness or a watch breaks during the traumatic incident. The longer the time since death, the greater the chance for error in determining the postmortem interval. There are numerous individual observations which, when used together, provide the best estimate of the time of death. The examiner must check the following: rigor mortis, livor mortis, body temperature, and decompositional changes. A thorough scene investigation is necessary. The environment is the single most important factor in determining the postmortem interval.

Rigor Mortis

1. Muscles begin to stiffen within 1 to 3 hours after death at 70 to 75°F.

2. A high fever or high environmental temperature will cause rigor to occur sooner.

3. Rigor will occur more quickly if the decedent was involved in strenuous physical activity just before death.

4. All the muscles begin to stiffen at the same time. Muscle groups, because of their different sizes, appear to stiffen at different rates. Stiffness is apparent

sooner in the jaw than in the knees. The examiner must check the jaw, then the arms, and finally the legs, to feel if the associated joints are moveable.

5. The body is said to be in complete rigor when the jaw, elbow, and knee joints are immovable. This takes approximately 10 to 12 hours at 70 to 75°F environmental temperature.

6. The body will remain stiff for 24 to 36 hours at 70-75 degrees F before the muscles begin to loosen, usually in the same order they stiffened.

7. Rigor is retarded in cooler temperatures and accelerated in warmer temperatures.

8. When the body stiffens it remains in that position until the rigor passes or the joint is physically moved and the rigor is broken.

9. The position of a body in full rigor can give an indication whether or not a body has been moved after death.

Livor Mortis (Blood Settling)

1. Livor mortis is the purplish-red discoloration of the body after death by the settling of blood.

2. Blood will settle in the blood vessels with gravity in the dependent areas of the body.

3. Some dependent areas will not be discolored because the bones underneath the skin will compress the skin against a hard surface and prevent the blood from settling in the capillaries.

4. Livor mortis is noticeable approximately one hour after death and becomes "fixed" in about 8 hours.

5. When livor is fixed, the color will not blanche under pressure and will remain in those areas even if the body is repositioned.

6. There may be a slight discoloration in the new dependent areas even though the blood remains fixed in the original position.

7. Fixed blood seen on a nondependent location indicates that a body has been moved after death.

8. Livor mortis will be visible until the body becomes completely discolored by decomposition.

9. Cold weather, refrigeration, carbon monoxide poisoning, and cyanide poisoning will cause the livor to be bright red.

10. Livor mortis is more difficult to determine in dark-skinned individuals.

11. Ruptured blood vessels may occur in dependent positions such as hanging. These ruptured areas are called Tardieu spots.

Body Cooling (Algor mortis)

1. After death, the body cools from its normal internal temperature to the surrounding environmental temperature.

2. Body cooling is not an accurate method of predicting the postmortem interval.

3. At an ideal environmental temperature of 70 to 75°F the body cools at approximately 1 1/2 degrees Fahrenheit per hour in the early postmortem period.

4. If a decedent's body temperature were higher than normal because of infection or physical exercise, 98.6°F (37°C) is not an accurate starting point.

5. The outside environment determines the rate of cooling. Cooling occurs more quickly in the cold and may not occur in hot climates.

6. If body temperature is measured at the scene it should be taken on at least two separate occasions before the body is moved.

7. A rectal or liver temperature is the most accurate measurement.
8. The environmental temperature should be recorded.

Eyes

If the eyes remain open after death, the will become cloudy within a few hours.

Clothing

The type of clothing may help indicate what the person was doing and the time of day at death.

Use of Gastric Contents (See Autopsy)

Determining Time of Death by Scene Investigation

Clues concerning the time of death may also be found at the scene either away from, near to, or on the body. Evidence such as the type of insects on the body, flora beneath the body, or objects from the decedent's residence may be contributing clues.

Insect larvae on the body can be collected and saved in alcohol. An entomologist will be able to determine, not only the type of larvae, but also its developmental stage. Each stage has a specific time duration which enables an entomologist to state how long the larvae have been present.Bear in mind, however, that this time estimate is only the time larvae were present on the body.

Flora discovered under or near the body may be helpful. A botanist may be able to examine the specimen, classify the type of flora and time of year it would normally be present, and determine how much time elapsed to reach that particular growth stage.

Information from the scene, other than that associated with the body, may also be critical in estimating the time of death. All clues from a house or an apartment must be analyzed. Was the mail picked up? Were the lights on or off? Was food being prepared? Were any major appliances on? Was there any indication as to the kind of activity the individual was performing, had completed, or was contemplating? How was the person dressed?

Decomposition

1. Decompositional changes are dependent upon the environment.

2. At moderate temperatures, decompositional changes won't occur for a day or two.

3. As rigor passes, the skin begins to turn green, first in the abdomen and then spreading to the rest of the trunk and body, however, this is variable.

4. As discoloration occurs, the body will begin to swell due to bacterial gas formation which is promoted in warm weather and retarded in cold weather.

5. When the body is bloated, the epidermis begins to slip, and the blood begins to degrade.

6. Subcutaneous marbling — degenerated blood visible through the skin.

7. Purging — decomposed blood and body fluids come out of the body orifices. This should not be mistaken for an injury.

8. Skeletonization — may take weeks or months depending on the environment. Many bodies are discovered in partial skeletonization.

9. Bodies may be more decomposed in areas where there are injuries because larvae are attracted to blood and they cause decomposition to occur more quickly.

Adipocere (ad-i-po-ser)

Fat tissue beneath the skin begins to saponify (turn into soap). This hardening, which takes a minimum of a few weeks to develop, will keep the body in a relatively preserved state for many months. Unlike normal decompositional changes, there is no green discoloration or significant bloating. The exterior of the body remains white and the outermost layers of the skin slip off.

For bodies totally submerged in cold water, adipocere will be evenly distributed over all body surfaces. Not all bodies having adipocere are found in water. For example, bodies found in plastic bags, which provide a moist environment, may also undergo this change. There may also be a differential development of adipocere depending on whether or not areas of the body are clothed.

Mummification

Mummification occurs in hot, dry environments. The body dehydrates and bacterial proliferation may be minimal. The skin becomes dark, dried, and leathery. The process occurs readily in the fingers and toes in dry environments regardless of the temperature. Most mummified bodies are found in the summer months. It is also common for this process to occur in winter months if the environment is warm. It is possible for an entire body to mummify in only a few days to weeks. Once a body is in this state, it can remain preserved for many years.

6

Decedent Identification

Positive Identification

Visual

Some jurisdictions require the next-of-kin to make the identification in person while others will alleviate some of the trauma to the family by allowing the family member to view a photograph of the face or body. Other jurisdictions suggest the relatives not look at the body until it has been prepared for viewing at the funeral home. Even though this method of identification is the easiest and most common, problems may be encountered. Numerous injuries and decompositional changes may have caused such severe disfigurement that the family may not be able to take a close enough look to make a positive identification.

Fingerprints

Little needs to be said about this method of identification because of the uniqueness of an individual's fingerprints.

Dental

Unless the decedent is edentulous, dental comparison is an excellent method for making a positive identification because most people have had some type of dental work. Many pathologists can make the comparisons, however, difficult cases should be analyzed by an odontologist. Many times decedents with a complete set of dentures can be identified. The technician who made the dentures may put some form of personal identification on the dentures.

X-rays

Antemortem studies can be used for postmortem comparisons. Both radiologists and forensic pathologists make these comparisons. A radiologist should be consulted if the case is difficult. X-rays of the skull and the pelvis tend to be the best for comparison. The skull has sinuses (cavities) in the forehead area which are specific for each individual. A chest x-ray is not as good as the skull and pelvis for comparison.

DNA Fingerprinting

All individuals, except identical twins, have different DNA sequences on their chromosomes. These DNA sequences can be broken down and studied by the use of enzymes. The procedures for performing these tests were developed in the 1980s, making them relatively new. Any material with cells containing DNA can be used for comparison. Blood, hair, semen, teeth, and other tissue may be used.

Presumptive Identification

Skeletal Remains

Skeletal remains are usually examined by an anthropologist, preferably a forensic anthropologist. They are expert in estimating age, gender, and race, and may use numerous scientific formulae to arrive at their conclusions. Age estimations are the most difficult to make; however this determination is becoming easier now that microscopic analyses are being performed.

Clothing

The style, size, and make of clothing are commonly used to make a presumptive identification. Relatives or friends may remember what the missing person was last wearing. Unfortunately, clothes will decompose along with the rest of the body or they can be destroyed if the body is burned.

X-rays

The location of antemortem x-rays does not ensure a positive identification. There may not be enough points of variation allowing the radiologist to render a conclusive opinion. A presumptive identification can be made if the x-rays are consistent with those of the decedent and there is no reason to believe the person is anyone else.

Physical Features

Tattoos, scars, birthmarks, the absence of organs due to surgical procedures and other physical anomalies are helpful in making identifications. The presence or absence of any of these characteristics may also be helpful in eliminating any possible matches, as well as in making a possible identification.

Circumstances Surrounding Death

Identification may be impossible to make based on the few remains discovered at the scene; however, the circumstances in which the remains are discovered may allow an identification to be made. For example, if only a few pieces of a body are located in a burned-out house, an identification cannot be made based on any scientific testing. However, if the owner of the house was last seen in the house, and if there is no reason to believe the remains are those of some other person, a presumptive identification of the owner can still be made.

7

Crime Scene Evidence Collection

Scene Investigation

Crime scene technicians, a medical examiner or investigator, and law enforcement detectives all take part in examining the scene for clues. The following is a list of different types of evidence that may be found at the scene, and how they are usually collected and preserved. Most of these items are usually collected by the crime scene technician.

Blood — Dried particles should be scraped into a dry container. Some dried areas may be sampled with a wet swab. The specimen should be dried before sealing it in a container. Articles of clothing or other objects containing blood may be submitted to a laboratory for a technician to remove.

Semen — The article of clothing should be collected or the specimen on the clothing can be lifted with water or saline.

Fingerprints — Soft objects containing an impression, such as clay, may be collected in their entirety. Prints on hard objects like glass or furniture should be lifted at the scene.

Firearms and other weapons — These should be submitted to a lab without special treatment at the scene. The technician must ensure proper handing so that fingerprints are not smudged or ruined. The pathologist performing the autopsy may need to see a suspected weapon for comparison with injuries on the body.

Bullets and cartridges — These should not be grasped with metal forceps because points of comparison may be damaged.

Hairs and fibers — These should be placed in separate containers and should not be crushed with a hard object such as metal tweezers.

Suspicious foods and pills — Each item should be placed in separate containers or bags to prevent contamination.

Footprints and tire marks — At the scene, casts should be made and close-up photographs should be taken.

Tool marks — There should be close-up photographs of the marks made by tools and, if possible, the damaged material should be removed for analysis by a lab technician.

Blood spatters — These should be photographed and described for analysis as to distance and angle of splatter. Samples may be removed for testing and preservation.

Other — Glass, soil, documents, cigarette butts, tobacco, and items thought to be involved in arson should all be collected and submitted to a lab.

Every scene should be diagrammed and photographed. Some jurisdictions are now using video in additions to still photography. Each item submitted to the lab should be referenced by either a photograph or written description as to its location in the scene. All containers with items submitted to the lab must be labeled with a case number, date, time, and name of the person who collected the specimen. Each specimen must have a chain of custody to determine who handled the specimen from the time it was initially packaged to the time it was stored after the analysis.

8

Signs of CPR and Treatment

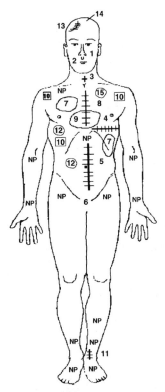

Figure 1. Signs of CPR (see next page for key).

Key to Figure 1.

1. **Nasogastric tube** (nose to stomach).

2. **Endotracheal tube** (mouth to trachea).

3. **Cricothyroidotomy and tracheotomy**

   The cricothyroidotomy is performed higher up on the neck than the tracheotomy. It should be located approximately 1 inch below the top of the larynx (Adam's apple). This procedure may be performed by EMT personnel at the scene because there are fewer complications than the tracheotomy.

   The tracheotomy is performed by a physician. It is an incision in the lower neck through the skin and airway (trachea) to establish an airway. This can be done emergently or as therapy for difficulty in breathing. This procedure is not performed out in the field, only in the hospital. The incision should not be confused with a stab or incised wound. Checking with the physician or the medical record will reveal who performed the procedure and when it took place.

4. **Thoracotomy**

   These are large incisions made into the sides of the chest, usually on the left side below the nipple. They are made in an attempt to remove blood and pump the heart manually.

5. **Laparotomy**

   An incision into the abdominal cavity to check for blood and injuries.

6. **Foley catheter**

   A tube to empty the bladder.

7. **Abrasions from electrocardioversion (shock)**

8. **Sternotomy**

   An incision into the chest and then through the sternum to get to the heart.

9. **Contusions from chest compressions**

10. **EKG patches**

11. **"Cut-downs"**

These are incisions in the skin made by scalpels. The objective is to locate a blood vessel into which a catheter can be inserted. Most of the time a catheter is in the blood vessel and held there by a suture. Occasionally, the catheter and the suture material are not present. These "cut-downs" are more commonly located over the ankles, wrists, and front of the elbows (antecubital fossae).

12. **Abdominal and chest tubes**

These tubes are usually on the sides of the chest or abdomen. They are used to evacuate blood from the cavities.

13. **Craniotomy**

This is a surgical procedure on the head to remove blood which has accumulated over the brain.

14. **Pressure monitors of the brain**

A tube is placed through the scalp and skull into the brain to monitor the pressure of the brain.

15. **Implanted defibrillators and pacing devices**

These small devices are surgically implanted under the skin in the upper chest. They may be done emergently in the operating room.

NP. **Needle punctures**

These are needle puncture site used for extracting blood and placement of intravenous catheters attached to fluid bags. Some of the catheters and fluid bags may still be in place.

In addition to those found in CPR, there may be larger needle punctures in the abdomen and in the lower legs (shins) of children. Large needles (trocars) may still be in place at the time of the autopsy.

Deaths in the Hospital

The following are common complications causing death following trauma and natural diseases. These complications are to be considered mechanisms and not causes of death.

Arrhythmias

Abnormal heart rhythms are common after stress from trauma or after a heart attack.

Infections

Infections may be localized (in one location) such as pneumonia or they may be systemic throughout the blood system (septicemia). These are common after burns.

Electrolyte Abnormalities

These are chemical problems in the blood. Potassium abnormalities, the most common, cause problems with proper heart functioning. These are common after burns.

Hemorrhage and Ruptures of Blood Vessels

Bleeding into the head and body after trauma are common.

Blood Clots

95% of the time blood clots form in the veins of the lower legs. They usually occur after an active person becomes immobile, such as after surgery. Sometimes blood thinners such as heparin and coumadin are given to prevent these clots. Death occurs when large clots break loose, travel up the legs, and go through the heart plugging up the major blood vessels feeding the lungs.

Shock

Shock occurs when blood vessels are no longer able to maintain normal blood pressure and organs die because they are not perfused with blood that carries oxygen.

Disseminated Intravascular Coagulation (DIC)

DIC occurs when the body is no longer able to clot blood normally. The smaller blood vessels begin to leak and the person dies of shock.

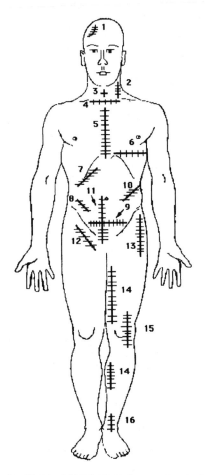

Figure 2. Signs of Old Surgery (see next page for key).

Key to Figure 2.

1. **Craniotomy**
   An incision into the skull.

2. **Carotid endarterectomy**
   The removal of atherosclerosis (hardening of the arteries) from the carotid artery.

3. **Tracheotomy**
   An opening into the trachea for breathing.

4. **Thyroid surgery**

5. **Sternotomy**
   An incision through the sternum to reach the heart for open heart surgery.

6. **Thoracotomy**
   An incision into the chest.

7. **Cholecystectomy**
   The removal of the gallbladder.

8. **Appendectomy**
   Removal of the appendix.

9. **Laparotomy**
   An incision into the abdomen.

10. **Nephrectomy**
    Removal of a kidney.

11. **Laparotomy (vertical)**

12. **Herniorraphy**
    Repair of a hernia (may be on one or both sides).

13. **Hip replacement**

14. **Vein removal**
    Veins used in coronary bypass surgery.

15. **Knee surgery**

16. **Cutdown scar** (see CPR key)

9

The Autopsy

General and Specimen Collection

The autopsy is conducted by a forensic pathologist or a pathologist who is knowledgeable about trauma and sudden death. All findings should be described in an autopsy report which is completed after the examination. A pathologist may dictate the findings at the time of the exam or document them on a worksheet and dictate them later. Injuries in suspicious case and homicides should be photographed. Some jurisdictions are also using video cameras. All information from a case must be retained in the decedent's case file for later review by all interested parties.

The most important information determined at the autopsy is the cause of death. The manner of death may not be obvious and scene investigation may be essential in determining the manner of death. Besides documenting signs of injuries and natural diseases, a pathologist must collect evidence which may be helpful in determining the manner of death.

Evidence which can be collected include:

1. **Blood** — Blood must be collected for drug screens, blood typing and DNA comparisons. Blood for drug analyses can be collected in any container, but one containing fluoride oxalate prevents clotting and contamination from bacteria. The blood should be refrigerated and may even be frozen, except for DNA

testing and blood group typing. Blood should be collected in every case because it is always better to have it and not use it than discover later that it was needed but never obtained.

2. **Urine** — Urine is good for screening many drugs, especially drugs of abuse. If a urine screen is negative, blood usually does not have to be analyzed, unless specific drugs not apparent on routine screening are suspected.

3. **Anal, vaginal, and oral swabs** — Cottons swabs are used to collect seminal fluid and sperm in suspected cases of rape. All swabs should be air-dried prior to packaging. Often, a swab may be made on a glass slide.

4. **Foreign material** — Hairs, threads, fragments of wood, metal, and any other foreign material should be collected in suspicious cases.

5. **Clothing** — Every article of clothing in homicides and suspicious cases should be dried and bagged. A pathologist should not cut clothing off a body in a suspected homicide. For example, if a pathologist cuts through the hole of an entry wound in a gunshot case, the hole will be distorted and future evaluation regarding point of entry or exit might be impossible.

6. **Hair**— Head hair samples are routinely taken in homicides. Pubic hair samples are submitted if a sexual assault is suspected. Hair samples should be taken from more than one site. Combings of the pubic hair in suspected sexual assault cases should be submitted separately.

7. **Vitreous humors** — This fluid is good for screening certain drugs, especially alcohol. It is also used to measure glucose and electrolytes, especially sodium, chloride, urea, and creatinine.

A pathologist may submit other fluids and organs from a body for drug testing as deemed necessary. Some labs prefer different tissues and fluids such as bile and brain. A pathologist usually knows the lab's preference.

Specimen ccollection is usually performed by law enforcement investigators. Ideally, crime scene technicians or their representatives attend the autopsy and help the pathologist collect further evidence. All evidence and specimens should be placed in separate containers. Each container is labeled with the pathologist's or investigator's name, date, autopsy number, and type of specimen. A chain of custody begins at this point and continues until the disposition of the specimen is completed.

The Procedure

After an extensive external examination a pathologist usually begins an autopsy with a standard "Y"- shaped incision. The short arms of the "Y" begin at the shoulders, meet at the breast and the incision continues in a straight line to the pubis. The skin is then reflected away from the chest and abdominal regions. The chest plate is exposed and removed by a saw. The pericardial sac is opened and blood is removed for toxicological studies here or in peripheral sites, such as the subclavicular or femoral vessels. The organs are then removed either en-bloc (Rokitansky method) or individually (Virchow method).

The brain is usually removed by an assistant. An incision is made from behind one ear and then extended across the top of the head down to behind the other ear. The scalp is reflected both forwards and backwards to expose the skull. The top of the skull is removed with a saw and the brain is exposed. The brain is removed and evaluated.

There is no one "best" method of performing an autopsy. The objective is to find the answer. A complete examination is recommended because a decedent may have more than one potential cause of death. For example, a person may have died from a ruptured aneurysm of the brain, but also have had terrible heart disease. If the brain were not examined because the heart disease was felt to be the cause of death, the diagnosis would have been missed.

The pathologist samples internal organs for microscopic examination when necessary. The cause of death is usually determined at the conclusion of the autopsy, i.e., at the end of the gross examination. However, microscopic analyses sometimes aid in diagnosing the specific cause of the disease, such as the types of cancer or infection. Microscopic analysis is not necessary in most cases, especially those in which trauma was the cause of death. However, if microscopic examination is performed, a final diagnosis is not usually rendered until the slides are reviewed. Some pathologists make slides on most cases, while others do not. There is no rule as to how often or how many microscopic specimens are taken.

Gastric Contents

The total volume and description of the amount of food, liquid, or other material present in the stomach should be recorded at autopsy. This information is more helpful in identifying the composition of the decedent's last meal, than it is in determining the time of the last meal. For example, a body is discovered dead in the evening, and only breakfast type food is present in the gastric contents. This finding would suggest that death occurred in the morning. The gastric emptying time is useful, however, only if taken in context with other information. In general, a light meal takes approximately two hours to pass through the stomach while a heavy meal might take up to six hours. This rule may be followed as a general guideline, but care must be used. Some foods such as celery or tomato skins take longer than meat or other vegetables to pass through the stomach to the duodenum. The rate of digestion is also dependent upon the mental and physical state of the victim prior to death. An excited person, threatened with violence, may have either a slower or quicker than normal gastric emptying time.

Chemical Analyses

The various components in the blood, cerebral spinal fluid, and vitreous humor have all been studied as a means to determine time of death. Unfortunately, none of the studies have been conclusive. Vitreous potassium has received the most attention over the years, but its use has been limited because of individual case variation.

The Report

A final autopsy report is generated when all the data including toxicology has been analyzed. There should be an injury section separate from other external findings. Reviewing a disorganized report would obviously be difficult especially if different kinds of information were buried randomly in various sections. A list of final diagnoses and opinions or comments should also be separate from the main body of the report. There should be no editorializing or interpretations in the body of the report, only in the opinion or comment section.

10

Other Experts Who May Be Needed

Accident Reconstructionist

These specialists are usually policemen, highway patrolmen, or forensic engineer who have advanced training in recreating motor vehicle accidents. They can determine the speed of a particular motor vehicle at the time of an accident and how vehicles react after impact. They may also determine a body's location in a vehicle prior to impact.

Anthropologist

Anthropologists study bones. They have a better than 90% chance of determining the race, sex and an age range in most cases. The more complete the skeleton, the greater the accuracy. Partial skeletons are much more difficult to evaluate. Some anthropologists specialize in facial reconstruction. They can construct facial detail from skull bones. Unknown skeletons have been identified by this specialized technique. Anthropologists, however, should not make a positive identification from bones alone unless there is other material available for comparison, such as an X-ray or a detailed medical report. Anthropologists have been known to evaluate specific bony injuries in order to help with determining cause of death.

Botanist

Botanists are able to look at plant material recovered from a scene or body and give some clues about a plant's origin. They know which plants are indigenous to particular areas. This information may help in determining if a body was transported from one location to another.

Crime Scene Technician

The job of the crime scene technician begins after the discovery of a body. This expert is a specially trained individual who is usually a member of local law enforcement or a state-wide investigative unit. The technician's expertise includes: (1) photographing and diagramming the death scene, (2) collecting all potentially important evidence in a investigation, such as blood, hair, fiber samples and weapons, (3) recovering fingerprints and other prints, such as those from shoes and tires, and (4) analyzing blood spatters.

Criminalist

The criminalist receives training in many different areas, such as questioned documents, ballistics, serology and toxicology. These areas are subspecialties in their own right. Most criminalists work in a laboratory with evidence such as blood, bullets, fingerprints, ammunition, and trace evidence, such as fibers and hair, soil, glass, and impressions left by other objects.

This expert can test a variety of other materials such as soil for its component elements and glass for its fragility and direction of impact. Footwear impressions, and tire treads can be matched with referenced manufacturers and retailers. Paint chips can be analyzed for their components and can be compared to the paint used by known manufacturers. Automobile manufacturers keep accurate records of the paint used on each make and model of their vehicles. Volatile liquids, such as gasoline or paint thinner, can be determined from suspected arson case.

Engineer

Engineers are experts in materials and forces acting upon different materials. They are involved in traffic accidents, impact injuries, trajectories of projectiles and many other technical areas. They can be useful in many different product liability cases and are important in civil as well as criminal cases.

Entomologist

Insects are this expert's forte. Entomologists can identify not only the type of insect at the scene, but the age of the larvae. They know which ones are prevalent at any particular time of the year and how long it takes before eggs are laid on a body. This information helps to show how long a body remained in a particular location, but it does not necessarily tell an examiner how long the person was dead. A person may have died in one location and then moved to another.

Forensic Pathologist

Forensic pathology, a subspecialty in pathology, is the study of how and why people die by natural and traumatic means. A physician who becomes a forensic pathologist first attends an approved pathology residency program and then trains in one of the approved forensic fellowship training programs throughout the country. After training, the pathologist is eligible to take an examination to become board certified.

Most full-time forensic pathologists work in either a medical examiner's or coroner's office located in larger cities. These offices may operate as separate departments or divisions of other city, county, or state agencies. These offices vary in jurisdiction in each state and usually investigate traumatic, sudden, unexpected or suspicious deaths. They are also directly or indirectly connected to crime labs which have experts in serology, trace evidence, toxicology, **and ballistics.**

Odontologist (Dentist)

A bite mark on a victim or an assailant can be matched to the person making the bite. An expert who can analyze and interpret this data is specifically trained to make these determinations. Prior to making molds and photographs of the marks, an odontologist swabs the area to remove any saliva. An offender's blood type can be determined if they are one of the 80% of the population whose blood type is secreted in their bodily fluids. An odontologist is also an important consultant when positive identification is required. Dental comparisons are useful when visual and fingerprint identification cannot be made.

Radiologist

The expertise of a radiologist is used frequently by a medical examiner's office. Comparisons of antemortem to postmortem radiographs aid in decedent identification. These analyses are very important when a decedent cannot be identified by fingerprints or dental exams. A radiologist is also consulted for the evaluation of bony abnormalities in cases of suspected child abuse.

Questioned Documents Examiner

These experts are able to analyze handwriting for comparison purposes. They can determine whether or not a suspect actually wrote the document in question.
Paper can be analyzed for its ingredients and age and ink can be analyzed for its chemical composition. Writing instruments, such as typewriters or pens, can also be evaluated.

Serologist

A serologist analyzes fluids removed from a scene: clothing, victim, and/or suspect such as blood, urine, or semen. If a specimen from a scene is not decomposed, it can be compared to a blood type of all parties involved in a investigation. Consequently, blood removed from weapons and other objects can be tested. Blood need not be fluid to be of value; dried specimens are still useful. Occasionally, specific typing cannot be performed and a serologist is only able to determine whether or not such blood is human. Many serologists are trained in the technique of DNA fingerprinting.

Toxicologist

The toxicologist evaluates organs and fluids from an autopsy and a scene for the presence or absence of drugs and chemicals. The types of pills or powders found on suspects can also be determined. Most common drugs of abuse and poisons can be readily discovered and quantitated. However, not every drug and chemical appears in a routine drug screen. The pathologist and investigator must consult with a toxicologist if any unusual drugs or poisons are suspected. They should also let the toxicologist know what prescribed or illegal drugs a decedent was taking. Drugs and medicines from a scene should be recovered for analysis if needed.

11

Cause, Mechanism, and Manner of Death

Cause

The cause of death is the injury or disease which begins the train of events that ultimately leads to death. The cause of death may be separated into a proximate cause and an immediate cause. The proximate cause is the initial event and the immediate cause is the last event prior to death. For example, a beam falls on the back of a man working at a construction site and he becomes paralyzed. As a result of the paralysis, he loses bladder control and becomes prone to develop urinary tract infections. Years after the accident he develops a particularly severe kidney infection, becomes quite sick, and dies. In this case, the proximate cause of his death is the injury which left him paralyzed. The immediate cause is the infection of the kidney (pyelonephritis).

It is important to note that the length of time between the proximate and immediate cause does not change the final diagnosis of cause of death as long as there is an unbroken chain of events between the two. The time frame may be minutes, days, or years. An excellent history and investigation are critical in determining the proximate cause of death, ensuring the train of events between the proximate and immediate cause are not broken.

Mechanism

The mechanism of death is the biochemical or physiologic abnormality resulting in death. The mechanism of death in the above case is septic (infection in the blood with symptoms) shock. Other mechanisms of death include arrythmias of the heart, shock, or exsanguination (bleeding). The mechanism of death is not the cause of death and should not appear alone on the death certificate. For example, in someone with a gunshot wound to the head, the specific injuries of the brain and resultant swelling (cerebral edema) do not need to be included on the death certificate. The cause of death is the gunshot wound to the head.

Manner

The manner of death is the circumstance surrounding the death. Traditionally the manner is classified as one of the following: homicide, suicide, accident, natural, or undetermined. In the above case of the man dying from sepsis as a result of the paralyzing injury, the manner of death is accident.

Appendix A

Medical Terminology

A

Acquired — not born with; developed after birth.

Adenoma — a benign tumor made up of glandular elements.

Adhesion — fibrous tissue (scarring) which connects one structure to another as a response to disease or injury.

Alopecia — loss of hair.

Alveoli — air sacs in the lungs.

Ambulatory — able to walk.

Anamnestic — history.

Anastomosis — a joining together.

Aneurysm — an outpouching of a blood vessel or structure.

Angina pectoris — chest pain without death of the heart muscle.

Angiography — an X-ray study of blood vessels by use of of dye.

Anoxia — no oxygen.

Antecubital fossa — the space on the arm in front of the elbow.

Antemortem — before death.

Anterior — in front of.

Anthracosis — black pigment from coal or cigarette smoke.

Anthropophagia — insect and animal eating of the body after death.

Arrhythmia — abnormal heart beat.

Arteriolonephosclerosis — small blood vessel disease of the kidney.

Artery — a blood vessel which takes blood away from the heart.

Arteriosclerosis — thickening of artery walls, "hardening of the arteries."

Ascites — accumulation of fluid in the abdomen.

Asphyxia — lack of oxygen in the blood.

Atelectasis — collapse of a lung.

Atherosclerosis — thickening of artery walls by fatty deposits.

Atrium — one of two chambers in the heart which accepts blood from either the lungs or the rest of the body.

Atrophy — wasting away.

Autolysis — degeneration of cells and tissues after death.

B

Benzoylecognine — a metabolite of cocaine.

Bifurcation — a division into two branches.

Bronchi — the breathing tubes between the trachea and the lungs.

Bronchioles — smaller divisions of the bronchi.

Bronchopneumonia — infection of the lung beginning in the bronchiole (smallest air tube).

C

Calcification — turning hard by the development of calcium.

Cancer — malignant growth.

Capillary — the smallest blood vessel which connects arteries and veins.

Carbohydrates — starches and sugars.

Cardiac — heart.

Cardiac tamponade — blood filling the pericardial sac and compressing the heart.

Cardiomegaly — increased size of the heart.

Cardiorespiratory — heart and lungs.

Cardiovascular — heart and blood vessels.

Cecum — the first part of the large bowel (colon) where the small bowel attaches and the appendix is located.

Cerebral — brain.

Cholecystectomy — surgical removal of the gallbladder.

Cholelithiasis — gallstones.

Chordae tendineae — the strings of tissue connecting the heart valves to the papillary muscles in the heart wall.

Cirrhosis — scarring of the liver complicating alcoholism

Colon — the large bowel, between the small bowel and the anus.

Coma — unresponsive condition.

Congenital — born with.

Congestion — accumulation of blood.

Conjunctiva — the thin membrane lining the eyelid and eyeball.

Connective tissue — the supporting tissue between structures.

Consolidation — becoming firm.

Contrecoup — opposite the point of impact.

Coronal — the plane across the body from side to side.

Coup — at the point of impact.

Cutaneous — skin.

Cyanosis — the dusky discoloration of the skin due to a lack of oxygen.

Cyst — a hollow structure with a lining that is filled with a liquid or a semiliquid substancethere is a retention of air because of dam.

D

Decubitus ulcer — an ulcer formed on the skin from pressure.

Dementia — loss of intellectual function.

Dermatome — the distribution of a nerve on the exterior of the body.

Diabetes mellitus — a disease in which the body cannot use sugar because insulin is not being adequately produced by the pancreas.

Diastolic — the lower of the two values in a blood pressure.

Dilated — expanded in size.

Distal — away from the point of insertion.

DNA (deoxyribonucleic acid) — the structural backbone of genetic makeup in chromosomes.

Duodenum — the first part of the small bowel.

Dura mater — the tough, thick membrane located between the brain and the skull.

E

-ectomy — excision of.

Ecchymoses — hemorrhages beneath the skin (larger than petechiae).

Edema — the accumulation of fluid in cells and tissues.

Electrocardioversion — an attempt at cardiopulmonary resuscitation by electrical shock.

Emaciation — generalized wasting away.

Emphysema — lung disease where age to the alveoli (air sacs).

Endometrium — the inner lining of the uterus.

Epidural — over the dura.

Esophagus — the structure connecting the mouth to the stomach (food pipe).

Etiology — the cause of a disease.

Exsanguination — marked internal or external loss of blood.

F

Fibrillation — very rapid irregular heart beat.

Fibrosis — scarring, commonly associated with liver and the heart.

Flexion — the act of bending a structure.

Forensic pathology — the legal applications to the field of pathology, study of the cause and manner of death and injury.

Foramen magnum — the hole at the base of the skull through which the spinal cord passes.

G

Gastrocnemius — the calf muscle.

Gland — a structure made up of cells which secrete a substance.

Glucose — sugar.

Granular — a "lumpy bumpy" surface.

Granuloma — a tumor-like growth caused by an infection.

H

Hematoma — a mass (collection) of blood.

-hemo — blood.

Hepatomegaly — increased size of the liver.

Hepatic — pertaining to the liver.

Herniation — the protrusion of a structure into another space.

Hyperglycemia — increased sugar (glucose) in the blood.

Hyperplastic — increased number.

Hypertension — high blood pressure.

Hyperthermia — increased body temperature.

Hypertrophy — enlargement.

Hypothermia — decreased body temperature.

Hypoglycemia — decreased sugar (glucose) in the blood.

Hysterectomy — surgical removal of the uterus.

I

Ileum — the third and most distal part of the small bowel.

Infarction — death of tissue from a lack of blood.

Inferior — below.

Inflammation — infection.

Infraorbital — below the eye.

Intercostal — between the ribs.

Interstitial tissue — the supporting tissue within an organ (not the functioning cell).

Intestines — the bowels.

Intima — the innermost structure.

Ischemia — decreased blood flow.

-itis — inflammation.

J

Jaundice — yellow discoloration of the skin from a buildup of bilirubin (a breakdown product of red blood cells) in the body.

Jejunum — the second part of the small bowel.

L

Laparotomy — surgical incision into the abdomen.

Larynx — voice box (contains the vocal cords).

Leukemia — cancer of the blood forming organs and cells.

Ligament — thick tissue joining bones and cartilage.

Liver mortis — settling of blood after death.

Lumen — the inside of a hollow organ or blood vessel.

Lymph — the clear fluid which drains from the body's tissues.

Lymphoma — cancer of the lymph system.

Lymph node — nodules of tissue along the lymph drainage system.

M

Mastectomy — surgical removal of the breast.

Mastoid — the area of the skull behind the ear.

Media — the middle layer of a blood vessel..

Medial — the middle.

Membrane — the lining tissue within a structure or between two structures.

Meningitis — inflammation of the coverings of the brain.

Mesentery — the structure which supports the intestines.

Metabolite — a breakdown product of a drug or chemical.

Mitral valve — the valve between the left atrium and ventricle in the heart.

Myocardium — heart muscle.

Myocardial infarct — death of the heart muscle from blockage of a coronary artery.

N

Necrosis — degeneration and death of cells and tissues during life.

Neoplasia — tumor or growth.

Nodules — raised skin lesions, may be benign or malignant.

O

Oophorectomy — surgical removal of the ovary.

P

Pancreas — the organ behind the stomach which produces insulin.

Papillary muscles — muscle bundles which control the heart valves.

Parenchyma — the functional tissue of an organ.

Penetration — into a structure.

Perforation — through a structure.

Pericardial sac — the sac surrounding the heart.

Perineum — the area of the body which includes the external genitalia and the anus.

Peritoneal cavity — abdominal cavity.

Peritoneum — the thick tissue lining the abdominal cavity.

Perivascular — around blood vessels.

Petechiae — pinpoint hemorrhages.

Pharynx — the structure at the back of the nose and mouth before the esophagus and larynx.

Pinna — the external ear.

Pleura — lining the lung or inside the chest.

Pleural space — space between the lung and the chest wall.

Posterior — behind or back.

Postmortem — after death.

Prone — lying face down.

Proximal — towards the point of insertion or the main part of the body.

Purging — the decomposed bodily fluids which come out the nose and mouth.

R

Renal — kidney.

Rigor mortis — stiffening of the muscles after death.

S

Sagittal — a plane across the body from front to back.

Salpingo-oopherectomy — surgical removal of the fallopian tubes and the ovaries.

Sarcoma — a malignant tumor of the soft tissue.

Septicemia — bacteria in the blood system with signs and symptoms of disease.

Shock — inadequate circulating blood volume because of either a loss or redistribution of blood.

Small bowel — the small intestine, extending from the stomach to the colon (large bowel).

Soft tissue — fat or supporting tissue.

Splenectomy — surgical removal of the spleen.

Stenosis — narrowing.

Subarachnoid — beneath the arachnoid.

Subcutaneous marbling — the black discoloration of the blood vessels on the outside of the body which appears during decomposition.

Subdural — beneath the dura

Subluxation — bones which partially slip out of join.t

Superior — above.

Supine — lying on the back with face upward.

Supraorbital — above the eye.

Suture — joints in the skull where the bones come together.

Syncope — fainting.

Systolic — the higher of the two valves in a blood pressure.

T

Tachycardia — fast heart beat.

Tardieu spots — small hemorrhages from ruptured blood vessels on the extremities which occur after the body has been in a dependent position.

Thoracic cavity — chest cavity.

Thoracotomy — surgical incision into the chest cavity.

Thorax — chest.

Trachea — (wind pipe) the structure between the larynx (voice box) and the bronchi.

Tricuspid valve — the valve between the right atrium and right ventricle in the heart.

U

Ureter — the structure which takes urine from the kidney to the urinary bladder.

V

Varix (Varices) — enlarged dilated vein from a backup of blood , often seen in alcoholics who have cirrhosis of the liver.

Vein — a blood vessel which returns blood to the heart.

Ventricle — a chamber containing either blood or fluid (e.g., the heart has two ventricular chambers).

Vitreous humor — the fluid in the eye which gives the eye its shape.

Appendix B

Prescription Medicines

Look up the drug in question alphabetically. The number associated with the drug determines its basic classification. For example: Heparin, 3. The "3" indicates heparin is an anticoagulant (a blood thinner). Capitalized drugs are brand names.

Classifications:

1. Analgesics
2. Analgesic (narcotics)
3. Anticoagulation (blood thinners)
4. Anticonvulsants (seizures)
5. Antidepressants
6. Antidiabetics
7. Antiemetic (vomiting)
8. Antihistamines (colds and allergies)
9. Anti-inflammatory (infections)
10. Antineoplastic (cancer)
11. Cardiovascular (heart and blood vessels)
12. Diuretics (fluid removal)
13. Hormones and synthetic substitutes
14. Laxatives and antidiarrheal
15. Miscellaneous and unclassified
16. Muscle relaxants
17. Nervous system, specialized
18. Sedatives and hypnotics (sleeping)
19. Tranquilizers
20. Vitamins

B

baclcofen, 16
Bactrim, 9
BCNU, 10
beclomathasone, 13
Benedryl, 1, 8
Benemid, 15 (gout)
benztropine,
betamethasome, 13
bisacodyl, 14
Bismuth, 14
Blenoxane, 10
bleomycin, 10
bretylium, 11
Bretylol, 11
Brevibloc, 11
Brevital, 18
bromocriptine, 15
brompheniramin, 8
Buspar, 18
buspirone, 18
busulfan, 10
butalbital, 18

C

Cafergot, 17 (migraine)
caffeine and ergotamine,
    17 (migraine)
calcitriol, 20
Capoten, 11
captopril, 11
carbamazepine, 4
carboplatin, 10
Cardene, 11
Cardizem, 11
Cardura, 11
carisoprodol, 16
carmustine, 10
Catapres, 11
Ceclor, 9
cefaclor, 9
cefazolin, 9
cephalexin, 9
Cephulac, 14
Cerubidine, 10
Chlor-Trimeton, 1
chloral hydrate, 18
chlorambucil, 10
chlorothiazide, 12
Chlorpheniramine, 1
Chlorpromazine, 19
chlorpropamide, 17
chlorthalidone, 12
cholestyramine, 11
Chronulac, 14
cimetadine, 15
Cinobac, 9
cinoxacin, 9
cisplatin, 10
Citroma, 14

Claritin, 1
Claritin, 8
Cleocin, 9
clindamycin, 9
clofazamine, 9
clofirate, 11
Clomid, 15
clomiphene, 15
clomipramine, 5
clonazepam, 4
clonidine, 11
cloxacillin, 9
co-trimoxazole, 9
codeine, 2
Cogentin, 17 (Parkinson's)
Colace, 14
colchicine, 15 (gout)
Colestid, 11
colestipol, 11
Compazine, 7
Cordarone, 11
corticotropin, 13
cortisone, 13
Cosmegen, 10
Cotrim, 9
Coumadin, 3
cromolyn sodium, 15
    (lung disease)
cyanocobalamin, 20
cyclobenzaprin, 16

cyclophosphamide, 10
cyclosporine, 15 (used
    in transplants)
cyproheptadine, 1
cytarabine, 10
Cytosar, 10
cytosine arabinoside, 10
Cytovene, 9 (viral)
Cytoxam, 10

D

dacarbazine, 10
dactinomycin, 10
Dantrium, 16
dantrolene, 16
daunorubicin, 10
Deca-Duraboline, 13
Declomycin, 9
Decradron, 13
demeclocycline, 9
Demerol, 2
Depakene, 4
Depakote, 4
desipramine, 5
desipramine, 4
desmopressin, 13
dexamethasone, 13
Dexedrine, 15 (stimulant)
dexrazoxane, 15
dextroamphetamine, 15
    (stimulant)

Leukeran, 10
leuprolide, 10, 13
levamisole, 15
Levarterenol, 17
Levophed, 17
levothyroxine, 13
lidocaine, 11
lindane, Kwell, 9 (lice)
Lioresal, 16
liothyronine, 13
lisinopril, 11
lithium, 15 (antimaniac)
Lomotil, 14
Loniten, 11
loperamide, 14
Lopressor, 11
loratadine, 8
lorazepam, 18
loxapine, 18
Loxitane, 18
Lupron, 10, 13

M

Macrodantin, 9
magnesiumhydroxide, 14
magnesium citrate, 14
magnesium sulfate, 14
Mandelamine, 9
mannitol, 12
Matulane, 10

Mazicon, 15
Mebaral, 4
mecamylamine, 11
mecaptopurine, 10
mechlorethamine, 10
meclizine, 7
medroxyprogesterone, 13
mefloquine, 9 (malaria)
Megace, 10
megestrol, 10
melphalan, 10
meperidine, 2
mephobarbital, 4
mesna, 15
Mesnex, 15
Metamucil, 14
metaproterenol, 15 (lung disease)
metformin, 6
methadone, 2
methazolamide, 11
methenamine, 9
methimazole, 13
methohexital, 18
methotrexate, 10 (also for psoriasis)
methyldopa, 11
methysergide, 17
metoclopramide, 15
metolazone, 12

metoprolol, 11

MetroGel, 9

metronidazole, 9

Mexate, 10

mexiletine, 11

Mexitil, 11

Micronase, 6

Midamor, 12

midazolam, 18

Midrin, 1

Milk of Magnesia, 14

milrinone, 1

Minocin, 9

minocycline, 9

minoxidil, 11

mitomycin, 10

mitoxantrone, 10

MOM, 14

Monopril, 11

morphine, 2

Motrin, 1

MSO4, 2 (morphine)

MTX, 10

Mustargen, 10

Mutamycin, 10

Myambutol, 9

Myleran, 10

N

nabumetone, 1

Nafcil, 9

nafcillin, 9

nalbuphine, 15

naloxone, 15 (counteracts opiate overdose)

nandrolone, 13

Naprosyn, 1

naproxen, 1

Narcan, 15 (counteracts opiate overdose)

Nebcin, trobamycin, 9

Nebupent, 9

nedocromil, 15 (inhaler)

Nembutal, 18

neostigmine, 15, (myasthenia gravis)

Neptazane, 11

Neurontin, 4

niacin, 20

nicardipine, 11

nicoinic acid, 20

nifedipine, 11

Nipride, 11

nitrofurantoin, 9

Nitrogen mustard, 10

nitroglycerin, 11

Nitrolingual, 11

nitroprusside, 11

Nitrostat, 11

Nizoral, 9

norepinephrine, 17

norfloxacin, 9
Normodyne, 11
Noroxin, 9
Norpace, 11
Norpramin, 5
nortriptyline, 5
Norvasc, 11
Novantrone, 10
Nubain, 15
Nydrazid, 9 (tuberculosis)

O

Oncovin, 10
ondansetron, 7
orciprenaline, 15 (lung disease)
Orinase, 6
oxybutynin, 16
oxycodone, 2

P

paclitaxel, 10
Pamelor, 5
pancuronium, 16
papavrine, 11
paracetamol, 1
Paraplatin, 10
paregoric, 14
Parlodel, 15
paroxetine, 5
Pavulon, 16

Paxil, 5
Pediazole, 9
penicillin, 9
pentamidine, 9
pentobarbital, 18
Pepto-Bismol, 14
Percocet, 2
pergolide, 15
Periactin, 1
Permax, 15
perphenazine, 19
Persantin, 11
Pertofrane, 5
Phenergan, 1
phenobarbital, 4, 18
phenoxybenzamine, 17
phentolamine, 17
phenylephrine, 17
phenylpropanolamine, 17
phenytoin, 4
phytonadione, 20 (K)
piperacillin, 9
piroxicam, 1
Plaquenil, 9 (malaria)
Platinol, 10
Plendil, 11
polymyxin B sulfate, 9
Pontocaine, 1
potassium iodide, 13
Pravachol, 11

Appendix C

Photographs

Discussion of the Photographs

1. **Identification.** This baby, whose body was discovered in a toilet, could not have been identified prior to the discovery of DNA fingerprinting. DNA was helpful in providing this child's identity.

2. **Identification.** This hand with the ring was the only part of the body that could be used for identification in this aircraft crash victim.

3. **Identification.** The antemortem skull X-ray (right) can be positively matched to the postmortem skull (left) by comparing the frontal sinuses (arrows).

4. **Livor mortis.** The blanched areas over this baby's face shows the baby died with his face down on the blanket.

5. **Livor mortis.** Blunt trauma can be distinguished from livor mortis by cutting into the area. An absence of bleeding in the tissues (lower) proves the discoloration is from blood settling and not trauma.

6. **Time of death.** (A) Rigor mortis. (B) If rolled over, this man's leg will remain flexed. If the room temperature is between 70 and 75°F, complete rigor indicates length of death of at least 12 hours.

7. **Time of death.** (A) The pattern of the bedding is stained on the man's legs. (B) This man has been

26. **Blunt head trauma.** Spectacle hemorrhages (raccoon eyes). (A) This child was struck with enough force to cause soft tissue hemorrhage without fracturing the skull. (B) This decedent was shot in the head. Orbital skull fractures caused these hemorrhages around the eyes.

27. **Stab wounds.** Excessive stab wounds or impact injuries (overkill) suggest that drugs or sex may have been involved in the killing.

28. **Stab wounds.** (A) A defensive wound may occur when the arms or legs are thrown upwards in protection. (B) Stab wounds through solid organs such as the liver, or in this case the heart, may indicate the weapon has a blunt angle (arrow).

29. **Stab wounds.** Wound angles aid in weapon determination. The white arrow points to a blunt angle and the black arrow points to a sharp angle, indicative of a weapon with a single sharp cutting edge.

30. **Incised wound.** This man was killed with a baseball bat. The assailant then tried to saw the victim's head off with a handsaw (arrow).

31. **Incised wounds.** (A) Multiple hesitation cuts on the neck of this suicide victim. (B) Multiple incisions of the face and neck, usually indicating a homicide.

32. **Child abuse.** Physical abuse. These injuries could not have occurred naturally.

33. **Child abuse.** Malnutrition. Starved babies or adults have virtually no fat under their skin (arrow) and have a "concentration-camp" look.

34. **Sudden natural death.** Abundant blood at the scene may be suspicious. In this case, however, the man died suddenly from a ruptured blood vessel, a complication of his chronic alcoholism.

35. **Sudden natural death.** The left leg is much larger than the right leg because blood clots have formed and plugged up the blood vessels. The woman died because a large clot broke loose and blocked the blood vessels to the lungs.

36. **Sudden natural death.** Not everyone drowns in the bathtub. This man died of a brain hemorrhage from a ruptured aneurysm.

37. **Shotgun wound.** This extensive chest defect was made by a shotgun slug.

38. **Shotgun wounds.** (Left) The shot to the abdomen indicates direction of the pellets up towards the left side of the body. (Right) Marked spreading of the pellets. Only two pellets entered the man's chest cavity and caused death.

39. **Firearms.** Tight contact wound. All of the gunpowder is in the depths and edges of the wound. The skin around the wound is abraded from being blown back against the muzzle.

40. **Firearms.** Intermediate wounds. Both victims were shot from a distance of less than three feet. There is stippling, but no soot.

41. **Motor vehicle.** Significant damage to the vehicle suggests the occupant died as a result of the accident (top). Little damage to the vehicle suggests the occupant died from natural causes (bottom).

42. **Motor vehicle.** This boy died because he was dragged under a truck for almost three miles. The arrow points to blood on the pavement which could be followed from the accident to the body. The only significant injuries were the deep, abraded injuries from resulting form the dragging.

43. **Motor vehicle.** Occupants may have pattern injuries from striking objects inside the vehicle (arrows)

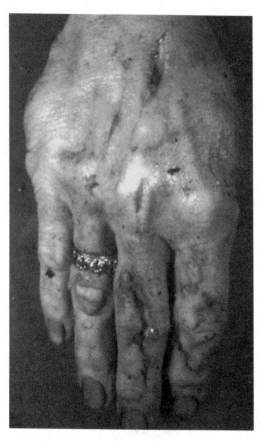

2. Identification. (see key)

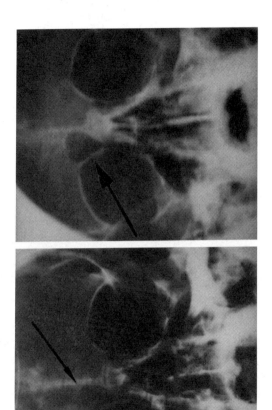

3. Identification. (see key)

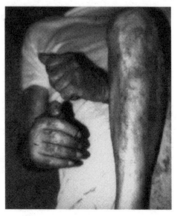

6. Time of death. (see key)

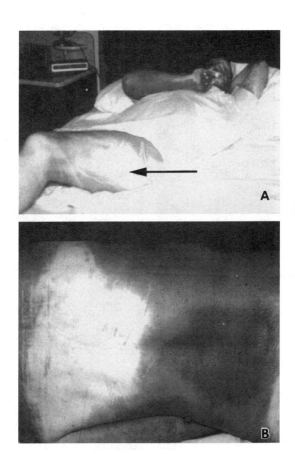

7. **Time of death.** (see key)

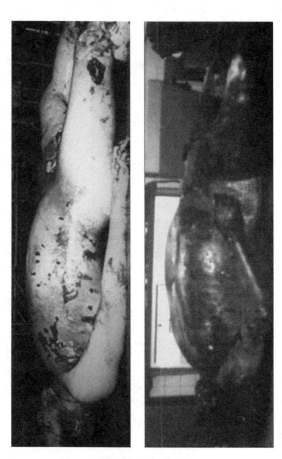

8. Decomposition. (see key)

9. **Differential decomposition.** (see key)

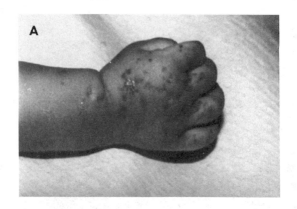

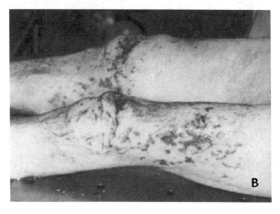

10. Anthropophagia. (see key)

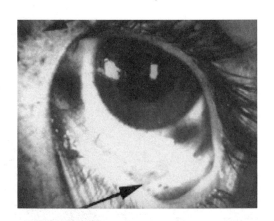

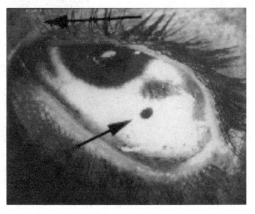

11. **Asphyxia.** (see key)

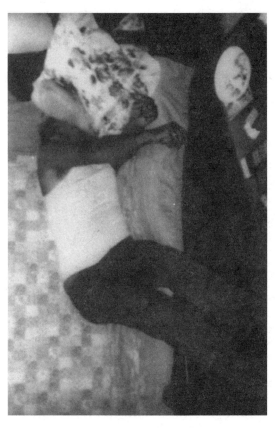

12. Asphyxia. (see key)

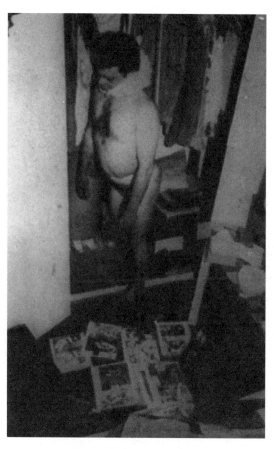

13. Autoerotic asphyxiation. (see key)

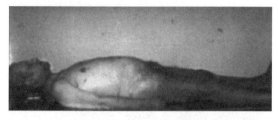

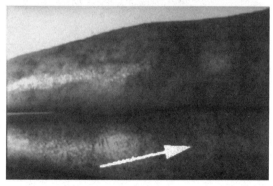

14. Asphyxia. (see key)

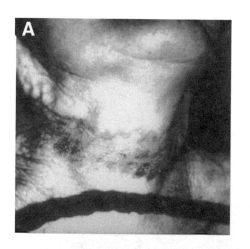

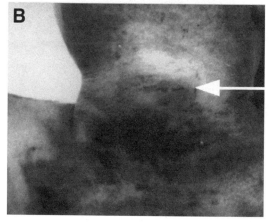

15. Asphyxia. (see key)

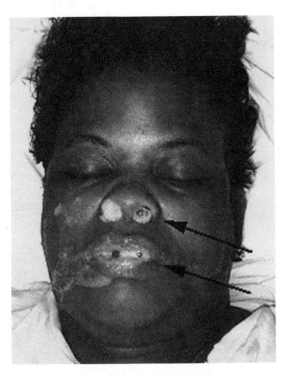

16. Drowning. (see key)

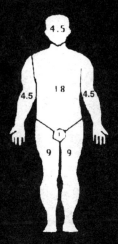

The Rule of Nines

The percent of total body burned is determined by adding up the numbers on the areas of the body which are burned

17. **Thermal injury.** (see key)

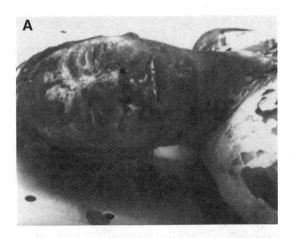

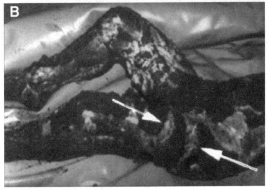

18. Thermal injury. (see key)

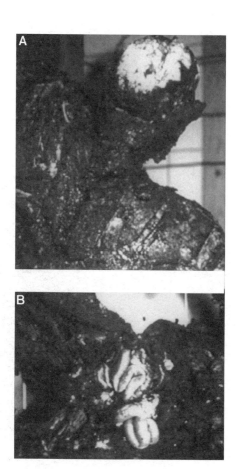

19. Thermal injury. (see key)

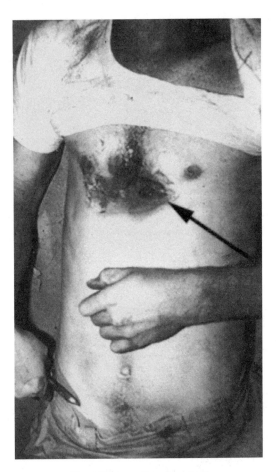

20. Electrocution. (see key)

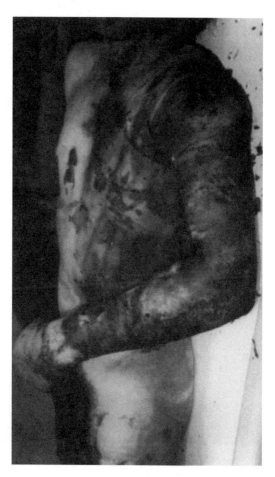

21. Electrocution. (see key)

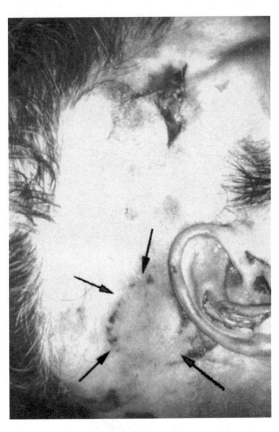

22. Blunt head trauma. (see key)

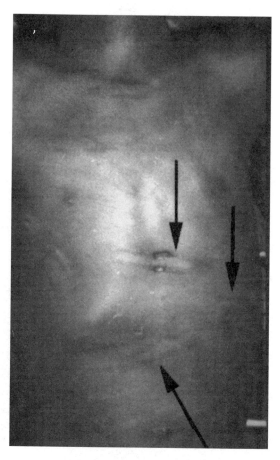

23. Blunt trauma. (see key)

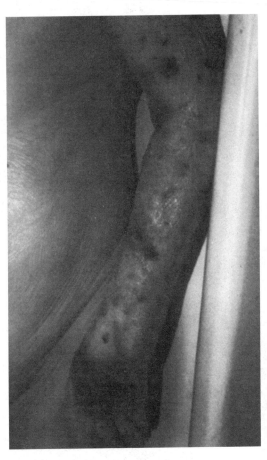

24. Blunt trauma. (see key)

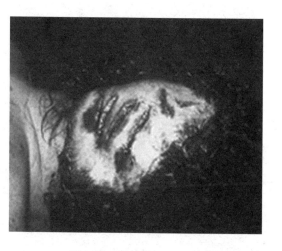

25. Blunt trauma. (see key)

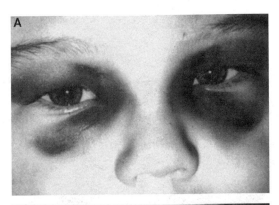

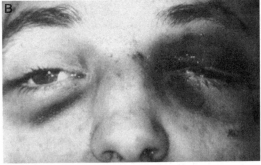

26. **Blunt head traums.** (see key)

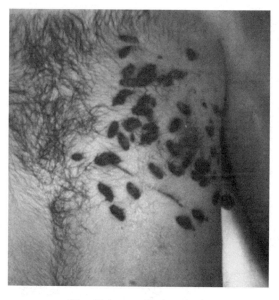

27. Stab wounds. (see key)

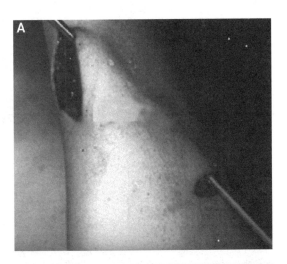

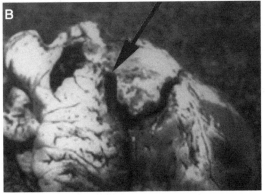

28. Stab wounds. (see key)

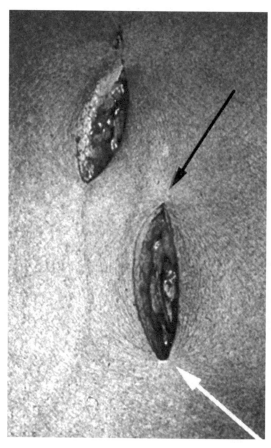

29. Stab wounds. (see key)

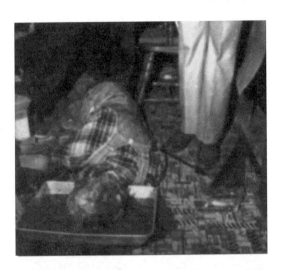

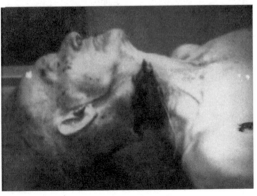

30. Incised wound. (see key)

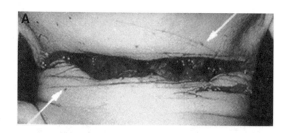

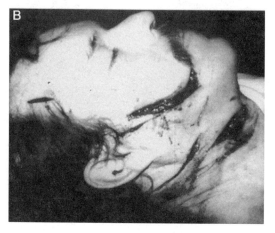

31. Incised wounds. (see key)

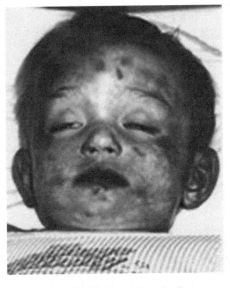

32. Child abuse. (see key)

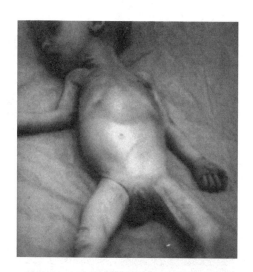

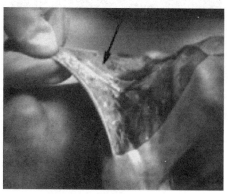

33. **Child abuse.** (see key)

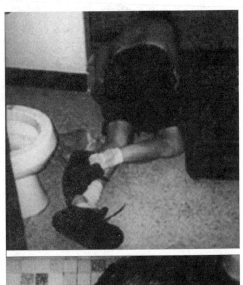

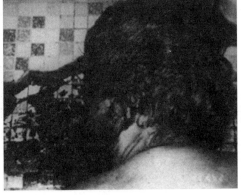

34. Sudden natural death. (see key)

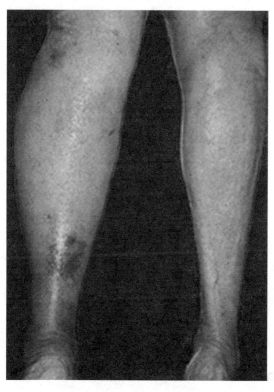

35. Sudden natural death. (see key)

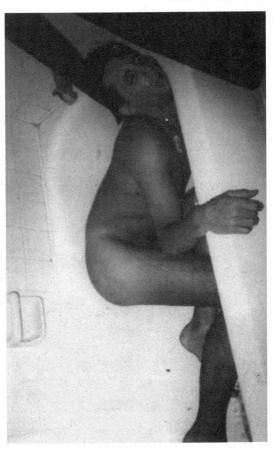

36. Sudden natural death. (see key)

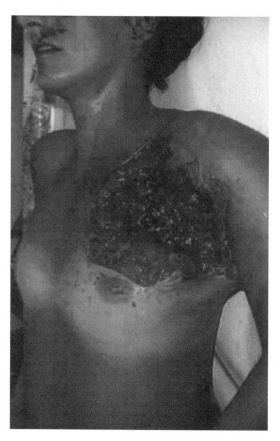

37. Shotgun wound. (see key)

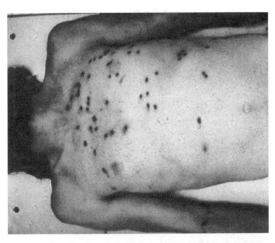

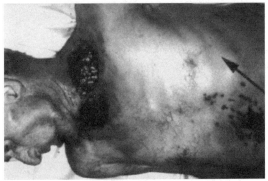

38. Shotgun wounds. (see key)

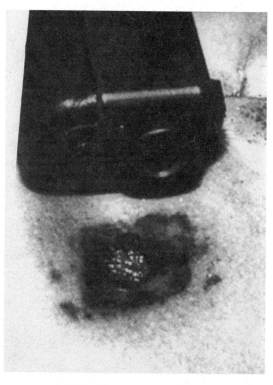

39. Firearms. (see key)

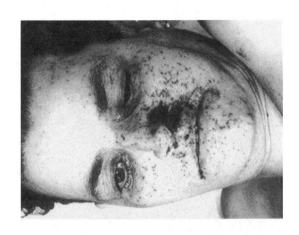

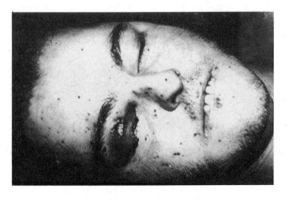

40. Firearms. (see key)

41. Motor vehicle. (see key)

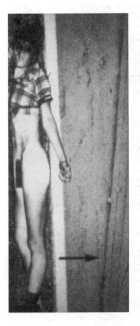

42. Motor vehicle. (see key)

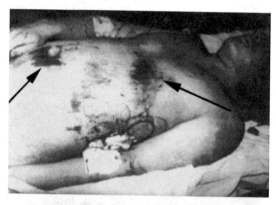

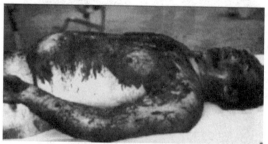

43. **Motor vehicle.** (see key)

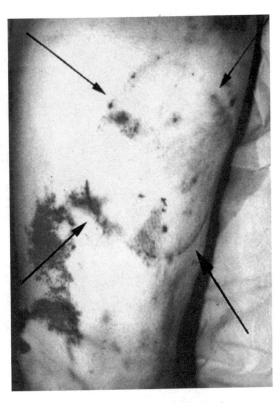

44. Pedestrian injuries. (see key)

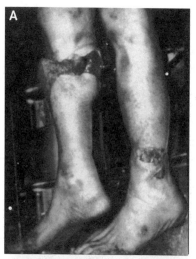

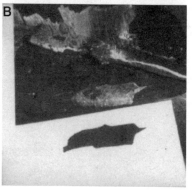

45. **Pedestrian injuries.** (see key)